Smoky Mountain Ghostlore

Juanitta Baldwin

Smoky Mountain Ghostlore

Juanitta Baldwin

Suntop Press
A Division of Suntop, Inc.
Kodak, Tennessee 37764
Virginia Beach, Virginia 23462

Printed and bound in the United States of America
First Printing 2005

Library of Congress Catalog Card Number: 2004097584

ISBN 1880308-26-6

From the Author

This book would not exist except for a series of serendipitous encounters with people who know magnificent tales of life in the Great Smoky Mountains, some in pre-television and pre-automobile days.

In those days, the region was a secluded enclave where the intricate skills of survival, self-sufficiency, heritage and culture were passed from generation to generation by word of mouth and demonstration.

Many of the events in this book cannot be explained with the knowledge that humankind has acquired. I resist the scientific bias that says anything that cannot be explained or replicated is either imaginary or invalid.

I respect science. I also respect the instinct, insight, and the invisible dimension of the human experiences.

I thank each person who contributed to this book by sharing experiences, photographs, and making suggestions. Above all I value those friends and associates for having a "reject index" that allows us to have a great time synthesizing new ideas and concepts without a commitment to embrace them.

This book is dedicated to
my cousins

Freida Stallcup Gilsdorf
and
Larry Spencer Stallcup

whom I admire for their track records of
vanquishing obstacles, trials, and tribulations,
and for the joy they shower into my life.

TABLE OF CONTENTS

Ghost Sounds

When the moon rides high up overhead...
and I am snug and warm in my bed...
in the eerie dark, the ghosts move round
making unique and scary sounds.

I listen to know when ghosts go by.
But I can't quite tell which I hear most...
a wail, the wind, or the clanging bell
of a feisty ghost.

Author Unknown

Chapter 1
Sapphire Valley's Twilight Ghost

Twilight in Sapphire Valley is a magical time. It is also the time that some people encounter the warm and gentle spirit of the Sapphire Valley ghost.

No human can be certain of his identity, but many believe that he is the Reverend Tom Hawkins, a seventy-three-year-old retired Methodist minister who walked into the twilight and vanished.

Twilight in Sapphire Valley — Courtesy Nathan Clay

About 5:30 on a blustery March afternoon in 1930, Reverend Hawkins' cow had not come down from the pasture on Timber Ridge. He told his daughter Ruth and her husband, Joe Wright, with whom he had lived since his wife died, that he was going to look for the cow.

As darkness descended Ruth and Joe became alarmed that he had not returned. He was very strong for his age, and more than enough time had passed for him to have located the cow.

Joe Wright went to the general store where men gathered to talk, and asked if anyone had seen his father-in-law. Several men said they had seen him heading toward Timber Ridge as the sun was going down, but no one had seen him since.

Reverend Hawkins' concerned family, friends and neighbors quickly formed a search party. They took their hunting dogs and searched Timber Ridge as best they could with lanterns and flashlights. They shouted his name, but the only responses were echoes. Exhausted, members of the search party agreed it was best to get some rest and begin fresh the next morning.

The search party started up Timber Ridge at first light, in a cold rain. They searched the trails, the undergrowth, the dangerous cliffs, and the coves, but at the end of the day they returned without a single clue.

No one gave a thought to the possibility that Reverend Hawkins had become lost because he knew every peak by name. The most plausible possibilities were that he had fallen and sustained an injury that made it impossible to walk, become ill, or been attacked by an animal.

Three days later five hundred rugged North Carolina mountaineers searched Timber Ridge and most of Sapphire Valley for two weeks, but they found nothing. The searchers were deeply troubled by the mystery. They, and Reverend Hawkins' family, hoped someone would solve it by discovering the body in a deep crevice, or in the dense undergrowth.

Almost eighty years have passed, and not one clue has surfaced to solve the mystery of how Reverend Hawkins vanished without a trace into the twilight.

Chapter 2
Wails at Cowee Tunnel

A 4-4-0 pulls a mixed train out of Cowee Tunnel on the Murphy
Branch of the Western North Carolina Railroad, circa 1892.
Photograph courtesy Matt Bumgarner

If you're close to Cowee Tunnel and hear *wails — the
sound of splashing water — rattling chains —* you are not
alone. People have been hearing these sounds since a
fateful winter day in 1883 when nineteen men, who were
working on this tunnel, died.

Cowee Tunnel is near Dillsboro, North Carolina. It was built in the 1880s by the Western North Carolina Railroad to open the formidable mountains to the outside world.

Finding enough workers who were willing to risk their lives to work on this very dangerous project was impossible, so the state of North Carolina supplied convicts from its prisons.

Cowee Tunnel was built to bypass a hairpin curve in the Tuckaseegee River, and the camp for the convicts was across the river from the tunnel. Each workday, the convicts were brought across the river by rafts and boats, under the watchful eye of a guard with a gun. They were shackled with heavy ankle irons, and chained together in work gangs of twenty.

On a cold winter day in 1883, the river was high and the swift current capsized one of the boats. All twenty convicts and their guard, Fleet Foster, were thrown into the icy Tuckaseegee River.

Nineteen convicts drowned. One convict, Anderson Drake, managed to free himself and rescued their guard, Fleet Foster. Drake might have been hailed a hero, but he stole Foster's wallet during the rescue. When it was found in his duffel bag, he was whipped and put back to work in the tunnel.

The bodies of the nineteen convicts were pulled from the Tuckaseegee and buried on top of a hill near the mouth of the tunnel. No one marked the graves, and the exact location of their mortal remains is uncertain. Perhaps their ghosts *wail*, *splash water*, and *rattle chains* to remind the world what happened to them.

Author's Note:

There are delightful train rides out of Bryson City and Dillsboro, North Carolina, these days on the Great Smoky Mountains Railroad. It steams across fertile valleys, spectacular river gorges, and *through Cowee Tunnel!*

For schedules, go to their Web site: http://www.gsmr.com, or call 1-800-872-4681.

Bryson City, North Carolina, depot — photo by Juanitta Baldwin

Chapter 3
McClary-Pollard Ghost

McClary - Pollard House

When I arrived at the McClary-Pollard house at ten-thirty on December 20, 2004, the sun was brilliant in a cloudless sky, and there was no breeze. The temperature was twenty-two degrees, so I was surprised to see the front door was open about ten inches.

I'd come to chat with W.C. and Glenna Julian about their ghost. Hoping nothing was amiss, I knocked on the door frame. Glenna came immediately, and she was almost as surprised as I was that the front door was open. After checking with W.C. to confirm that the door had been closed that morning, they concluded that the ghost was pleased I was going to write about his or her presence, and opened the door. This has happened before.

The Julians have no clue as to the identity of their ghost. They are the fifth family that has lived in the McClary-Pollard house, and as far as they can determine there have been no violent events within its walls.

Payne McClary and Mary Ann Lonas were married in 1840, and moved into this house. Doctor Fuquary Pollard bought it in the late 1800s, and it remained in his family until 1959, when it was sold to Ted Corbett. He sold it to Bobby Shepherd in 1967. Glenna and W.C. bought it from Shepherd in 1971, and have spent many hours renovating it and planting extensive herb gardens.

A few days after moving into the house, the Julians heard someone walking across the upstairs floor. All the family was downstairs. A search confirmed that no one was upstairs, but there was nothing to explain what they'd heard. It was puzzling, but they did not think they'd moved in with a ghost until several months had passed.

During those months, the sounds of objects falling to the floor, footsteps, and an open door that had been locked, gave them the option of choosing between the thought that it was collective hallucinations or a ghost. The choice was passive, but the ghost was gradually accepted as a member of the household.

The ghost has materialized for only one person. The Julians' daughter-in-law's sister was visiting, and slept in an upstairs bedroom. During the night she awoke, and a figure was standing at the end of the bed. Scared out of her wits, she hopped out of bed. The figure evaporated, and she is convinced she saw the McClary-Pollard ghost.

The Julians still hear footsteps, and objects falling. There has never been a pattern, or season of the year, when the ghost steps up its activity. I found it remarkable that the Julians long ago learned to distinguish between sounds the ghost makes and sounds made by members of the household.

If they discover that the source of the sounds is not a ghost, they fear it will not be as interesting.

Chapter 4
A Happy Ending Ghost Story

If you like stories with happy endings, you will love this one. It's Marlo Riddick's story, and here it is in her own words:

I found this decanter stored away in an old trunk in the attic of my grandfather's home in Smokemont, North Carolina, when I was sorting things to help him get ready to sell it. My curiosity lurched into high gear, because it was so unlike anything else in his home, and as many times as I'd been there, I'd never seen it.

The markings on the decanter established that it was made in Italy. It is covered in red leather, with a lovely green glass liner, and in perfect condition.

My grandfather seemed a bit embarrassed when I asked him about it, but after some gentle prodding he told me how he got it.

In the fall of 1949 he was working for a construction company with a contract to repair some of the buildings, and demolish others, in the abandoned Civilian Conservation Corps (CCC) camp near Smokemont.

My grandfather was assigned to check the inside of one of the buildings that was to be demolished, and salvage any papers, pictures and objects. The contractor had told the crew that a professor at a nearby college had asked him to do this because he was writing a paper on the CCC, and something might be found that would be significant enough to include in it.

The building had been a barracks. He found calendars and pin-ups on the walls, and two dusty cardboard boxes in a closet. One box contained CCC uniforms and boots, the other was filled with books and letters, yellow with age, and the red leather decanter. He put everything in the box for the professor, except the decanter.

He took it home with the intention of giving it to my grandmother, but he got cold feet because he was afraid she'd think he'd stolen it, and nag him to take it back to the job. That would not happen because, the way he figured it, he had as much right to the decanter as the professor did. He packed it away, thinking that if the time was ever right he'd show it to her. The time was never right before she died, and he told me it was mine if I wanted it. I took the decanter home, polished it and placed it on the mantel over the fireplace in our family room.

That evening Fred, my husband, noticed the new addition and admired the workmanship, and asked if I'd bought this new treasure at one of my frequent stops at garage sales. I told him the story, and we chuckled about Grandpa hiding it from Grandma.

A couple of weeks later, in mid-afternoon, I was in the family room working on the computer. Before we retired and moved to Smokemont, Fred and I had had successful, but stressful, jobs in New York City. Fred worked for a broker, and I was a research assistant for ABC News. Occasionally I'll get an offer from ABC to do a research job, and I was completing one on this day.

I glanced at the clock on the mantel, which is next to the decanter, and was startled to see an aura around the decanter. Thinking it was a reflection from the sun, I closed the drapes. It was still there. I picked up the decanter, and moved it to several locations in the house, but the aura remained visible.

The aura disturbed me a bit, and probably would have scared me out of my wits if I had not done extensive research on Kirlian photography. It is a photographic process that captures auras of people and objects invented by Seymon Kirlian. There seems to be no evidence that Kirlian photography results in a paranormal phenomenon, so I concluded that electrical conditions in the atmosphere had been just right to produce auras. Many people claim they can see them with their naked eyes, but I had doubted that until this afternoon.

I've always been fascinated with folklore and ghostlore. A week later I saw an ad for this type of seminar at Western Carolina University in nearby Cullowhee, and promptly enrolled. The sessions were lively, and I came away with a genuine appreciation of the region's rich heritage.

Perhaps thinking about ghosts ignited my imagination, but when I saw a young man standing in front of our mantel holding the decanter, my first thought was that I was looking at one. Before the Cullowhee seminar, I would have thought I was looking at an intruder. When I spoke to him he vanished, and that confirmed it for me.

When my brain connected the ghost with the aura I'd seen, I broke into a cold sweat, and a hurricane of thoughts zapped all my energy. After a couple of cups of strong coffee, I decided that maybe I was supposed to return the decanter to its owner, if he was still alive, or to his heirs.

I told Fred that I was going to try to find the decanter's owner, but omitted the real details of my motivation. He is supportive of my research, and remarked that perhaps we'd travel to an exotic, faraway place to meet the owner.

Finding the owner's son was one of the easiest searches I've ever done. I began my search on the Internet, and within seconds found the National Association of Civilian Conservation Corps Alumni (NACCCA) Web site. They have a museum and research center in St. Louis, Missouri.

Their online database listed many CCC projects in the Smokemont area between 1933 and 1935. This gave me a time frame. I found the lists of CCC enrollees who had been at Smokemont at the National Archives in Washington, D.C.

It seemed logical to search for the names of the CCC enrollees with Italian names.

I learned years ago that genealogical societies are gold mines of information, so I went to every genealogy Web site I could find and posted a query. I also went back to NACCCA, and a couple of volunteers scanned the lists and contacted likely CCC members who were still living.

Six weeks after I had begun my search I received an email from Victor Rizzuto:

"I have been contacted by a member of NACCCA, who tells me you are looking for a man who served in the CCC at Smokemont, and may be the owner of a decanter that was found there.

"My father, Emanuel Rizzuto, now deceased, served at Smokemont, and did have a decanter. He told the story many times about how his mother packed it in his bag when he was leaving for camp, with strict instructions that he take a sip or two of wine each day to help his body cope with the strange food he'd have to eat. It almost got him sent back home, because alcohol was banned in the CCC camps. Fortunately for him, one of the officers was Italian, and he persuaded the top officer that wine is part of the meal in Italian homes, and not consumed to get drunk. He was ordered to pour out the wine, but allowed to keep the decanter if he promised never to fill it in camp.

"My father said he kept his word, and would have brought the decanter home with him, but he was in a logging accident. His leg was broken, and after being hospitalized in Asheville, he was sent home. He wrote to several of his buddies asking them to send his things, but nobody did.

"Of course, I have never seen the decanter, but I have several pictures of my father's large family having meals. There are two with a decanter clearly visible. The pictures are old and faded, but I can have a professional duplicate and enlarge them, then send them to you for comparison with the decanter you have."

I was jubilant! I emailed Victor Rizzuto immediately, and in due time the pictures arrived. The decanter on the table was identical to the one on my mantel. It is now back in the Rizzuto family.

I'm pondering this experience, and probably will for the rest of my time on planet Earth.

Chapter 5
The Man at the Top of the Steps

Two Honeycutt brothers, Dan and Arthur, and their families pushed into the Cataloochee Valley in about 1830, which is on the North Carolina side of Great Smoky Mountains National Park. Most of their descendants lived there until they were forced to move in the late 1930s to make way for the park.

Before it became part of the park, this isolated valley was a prosperous settlement. Today, touring visitors can see preserved farm homes, barns, outdoor privies, springhouses and churches.

Lonas and Hester Honeycutt stayed in their home until the last day permitted by the park. They bought a small farm just outside the park boundary, but they were never as content after the move, even though they had a more modern and comfortable house.

Their son Gabriel and his wife, Lissie, managed a motel in the nearby town of Dellwood. The motel closed during the winter, so to supplement their income Gabriel started offering guided hikes through the Cataloochee Valley.

The valley is surrounded by rugged 6,000-foot mountains, so he could cater to those who wanted a short walk beside a rippling stream, or moderate to strenuous hikes, to enjoy the abundant wildlife and spectacular views.

The hike across the Honeycutt farms became one of the most popular, because Gabriel could tell true stories of the life his ancestors had lived. For a few years the hikers could look inside the homes and outbuildings. None of the Honeycutt buildings were on the Park's preservation list. The buildings fell into disrepair at a surprisingly rapid rate, and an assortment of animals took up residence, so inside tours had to be discontinued.

Gabriel's father, Lonas, would go along occasionally. He left most of the storytelling to Gabriel, but he loved to show hikers around the springhouse on the farm where he had lived for over forty years. He'd tell them how the logs had been put in place, and how he and his bride, Hester, had laid the rock steps up to the springhouse because she hated to walk up a muddy bank.

Gabriel Honeycutt was drafted into the Army in 1943, and served until shortly after the end of World War II in 1945. When he returned, the motel business was booming. The motel owners built two huge motels for him and Lissie to manage, and he did not resume the hikes.

He did make time to hike to the old home place with Lonas as long as he was able. Lonas died in April 1949. Before his death, Lonas had requested permission from the national park to be buried in the family cemetery on his farm, but his request was denied. The cemetery would be preserved, but no additional burials were permitted.

On a day off in June 1951, Gabriel hiked to the Honeycutt lands. All the buildings were gone, and the only visible sign of human habitation was the rock steps to where the springhouse had stood.

Photograph by Juanitta Baldwin © 2005

He had brought tools to clear the weeds from the cemetery. The task was not as formidable as he'd expected, because the trees and encroaching undergrowth had controlled weed growth.

This done, he photographed all the graves, the springhouse steps, and the few roses that were blooming in the space that had been his mother's garden. He sat down, leaned back against a giant oak tree to rest before hiking home, and promptly went to sleep.

When Gabriel awoke, he looked up, and saw his father sitting on the top step. It could not be, but there he was, sitting with his elbows on his knees, looking out over the farm he loved so dearly.

A cold sweat seized his body, and the hair on the back of his head stood up. He knew there were no such things as ghosts, so maybe he was having a dream.

After standing up, Gabriel remembered that his father had said he'd go back to the Chataloochee Valley, even if he had to go as a ghost. His fear evaporated, and so did the man on the top step.

Gabriel never saw his father sitting on the steps again, or anywhere else, but he has had several reports from hikers who said they saw a man on a set of rock steps.

The first report was in 1953. Three male students from Duke University were staying at one of the motels he managed. They were studying with Dr. J.B. Rhine, who was conducting studies of extrasensory perception and psychic phenomena. Their assignment was to visit places where people had been forced against their will to leave, and observe any unusual sights and sounds.

All this was new to Gabriel, so he asked if they were ghost hunters. No, the leader explained, we apply scientific methods toward the exploration of extrasensory valid human capabilities, and it has been established that some people can sense the presence of people and events from the past.

Prior to their first field trip Gabriel shared much of his family history with the students, but did not tell them he'd seen his father on the springhouse steps.

When they returned, the students told Gabriel that one student had seen an elderly man sitting at the top of some rock steps, and they had recorded many sounds. They hoped subsequent analysis back at the university would establish most of them as paranormal for a forest without human habitation.

Gabriel was tempted to share his experience of having seen his father, but decided against it because he did not want to participate in any of Dr. Rhine's studies.

Somehow he felt vindicated by this report, and those that followed, because he had been in doubt that he'd seen his father at the top of the steps. He'd almost persuaded himself that it had been a dream, but reports from others let him put the whole thing into the back of his head, where he keeps a file labeled "Unexplained."

Chapter 6
Lydia — Ghost of Greenbrier

The Greenbrier Restaurant in Gatlinburg, Tennessee, has exquisite cuisine, and a beautiful young ghost named Lydia.

Photograph by Juanitta Baldwin © 2005

I'd heard Lydia's story shortly after moving to Tennessee, and decided it was *the place* to entertain my three out-of-town guests. Two of them love ghost tales, and the third is a whodunit buff.

The legend is that Lydia lived at Greenbrier Lodge, which is now the Greenbrier Restaurant, off Highway 321 North in Gatlinburg. She was young and in love with a handsome young man to whom she was engaged to be married.

On the day set for the wedding, Lydia dressed in her long white wedding gown and went to the church. Hours passed, but the groom did not arrive. Being jilted was more than Lydia could bear. She returned to the lodge, climbed the stairs to the second floor landing, threw a rope over a rafter and hanged herself.

Several days after her death, the handsome man for whom Lydia had taken her own life was found dead in the Great Smoky Mountains. He had been mauled to death by a wild mountain cat. Some of those who knew Lydia said that after death her spirit had temporarily become a cat, and that she killed the love of her life for revenge.

Shortly after Lydia's death, her ghost began to roam through Greenbrier Lodge. A caretaker at the lodge relates that he was kept awake at night by Lydia crying out, "Mark my grave, mark my grave."

After many sleepless nights, he heeded her pitiful plea, and marked her grave, and never heard her cries again.

Guests at the Greenbrier Restaurant report seeing her wandering around, often on the second floor landing where she hanged herself. Other guests do not see her, but claim to feel her chilling presence.

On http://travel.yahoo.com, people post comments about places they visit. This comment about the Greenbrier Restaurant was posted on July 24, 2004, by "Scared ******** from Tennessee: "This place is severely haunted! I saw the ghost in the men's room. It was a woman, and she was transparent. She reached out for me, and I almost had a heart attack. They need to put a warning sign or something."

The weather on the October evening we headed for the Greenbrier was standard ghost story stock — intermittent rain, moonlight and fog. The restaurant is on Newman Road, which is a narrow ribbon of asphalt that winds through heavy woods to the top of a steep hill.

The Greenbrier does not accept reservations, but the waiting line was short. A jovial couple in front of us asked if we knew whether or not ghost appearances were added to the tab. My friends were nonplussed, because I'd kept mum about Lydia. The couple gave them a quick and accurate synopsis of Lydia's story.

We were seated upstairs, where floor-to-ceiling windows ring the dining area. The meal was delightful. High wind drove rain across the glass, offering temptation to take on substance in the imagination.

The jovial couple came by our table and said they thought they'd seen Lydia in the windows. We shared their enthusiasm, and expressed disappointment that no one in our party caught a glimpse, or felt the presence, of Lydia.

Chapter 7
Invisible House on Old Smoky

In the thirtieth year of time, the Bible tells us, Ezekiel looked up and saw "a wheel a-turning, way up in the middle of the air." The wheel he saw was invisible to other people.

In the twentieth century of time I, Ezekiel Byrd, looked up on Old Smoky and saw a house that is invisible to other people.

Why my Maker endowed me with the vision to see a house that is invisible to other people *is a mystery that neither I, nor my scientific friends, can explain.*

I don't know if Ezekiel saw the wheel more than once, but I see the house every time I go up on Old Smoky. If the faithful have got it right and we live on in another sphere called heaven, I intend to find Ezekiel and compare notes.

Had I been offered a choice, I might not have chosen to see the invisible house. Although to be honest about who I am, odds are that I would have been intrigued by the opportunity to experience things most of my fellow humans are denied, and opted in.

If I'd been born into a family where paranormal abilities are accepted as ordinary, my ability to see the invisible house would have been a minor ripple on the pond of family life, but in my conservative family it was a tsunami!

The house that I see is on Old Smoky, a 1000-acre mountainous farm in East Tennessee, between Ducktown and Turtletown. When I was a child, it was the home of Thaddius and Naomi Byrd, my paternal grandparents.

In 1940, my grandparents divided the land, and deeded a farm to each of their three sons, Caleb, Charles, and Luther, and their daughter, Callie. The three sons lived on their farms with their wives and children. Callie joined the

Navy and made it her career. She built a home on her farm and spent time in it each year.

This arrangement made for an extended, clannish family, and it was ruled by my paternal grandparents. Their decrees were carried out most of the time without question. There was occasional grumbling, a spat now and then, but never a serious thought of an insurrection!

Caleb, who is my father, and Charles are identical twins. I am an only child, and lived with my parents, on our farm, until I was twenty-two.

Understanding that the house I see is invisible to other people came about gradually.

My earliest realizations that other people did not see what I saw came about during play time with other kids. I often "hid" in the house during games of hide and seek. The other kids always found me, and I remember being confused as to how they could see me inside the house. They laughed at me for saying I was in the house, because there was no house there — anybody could see that!

My mother, Myssi Byrd, tells me that her first memory of my "seeing" the invisible house was when I was about three years old. We were sitting in a swing on the back porch at my grandparents' home on a rainy afternoon. Mother says that I pointed toward the yard and said, "That lady will get wet before she gets in the house."

I do not recall talking about the invisible house or the people around it any more than I recall talking about anything else, but my family does.

Early on, while the family was lamenting about my "overactive imagination" and "predisposition for lying," my great-great-grandmother, Clementine Byrd, cautioned them, and me, that I might have "the gift of second sight."

She reminded them that there had been a house behind my grandparents' house exactly where I "saw" it. It had

burned about a week after I was born. She believed God in His wisdom was showing it to me for some purpose, and if they interfered, they would place themselves in peril.

I've been told that to buttress her position she read them the passages from 1 Samuel 28 from the Bible about the Witch of Endor. In this account, King Saul asked the Witch of Endor to contact someone in the grave, the dead Samuel, so that he could ask him how he could gain a victory over his enemies, the Philistines.

She brought Samuel to King Saul. He asked Samuel what to do. Samuel told him that God was displeased with him for not doing what He wanted him to do, and that "tomorrow shalt thou and thy sons be with me." It came to pass just as Samuel had said. King Saul died for his transgressions, but the Witch of Endor was not harmed.

The lesson here, she told them, was that God endows some of His creatures and people with powers beyond human understanding, and that those without such powers should not try to thwart the exercise of those powers.

From the get-go, the family ignored Clementine's caution, and most of them divided into two camps, much to my parents' dismay.

The minority-camp members were the devout, religious zealots in the family, but were the most active and vocal.

They lamented about my "overactive imagination" and "predisposition for lying," and tried to convince my parents that I was under the influence of Satan.

The majority camp practiced religion from habit or social conformity. They secretly flirted with fortune telling, the zodiac, astrology, witchcraft, ghosts, and the like, and surreptitiously explored them for explanations of my behavior.

My parents refused to be persuaded by either camp, and did everything they could to protect me from being the object of curiosity, teasing, ridicule and condemnation while I was a young child. This was no easy task while trying to keep peace with our big, extended family.

Neither parent was ever unkind to me, but the invisible house was a barrier between us. As the years went by, my adaptive behavior was to gradually stop talking about the invisible house. The activity, and interest, within the camps has waxed and waned during the years, but at times it is still a very lively topic of conversation among us.

Few people outside the immediate family and close circle of friends knew that I claimed to see a house that other people could not see. By the time I was a junior at the University of Tennessee, it was on the back burner of my life until I fell in love with Samantha Alexander.

When I was sure I wanted to spend my life with her, I felt obligated to tell her about the invisible house before I popped the question.

I planned for weeks on how to break this to her without coming across as a nut case. The perfect opportunity came when my grandparents went to California for a month. We drove to Old Smoky and I showed Samantha around the farm, then we sat in the same swing on their back porch where my mother remembers my jabbering about the invisible house for the first time.

I'd spent hours trying to devise the best way to tell her about what I'd come to accept as "my paranormal sense," but came up empty. Knowing that this was probably my best opportunity, I decided to go straight to the point.

I recall my voice sounding strange when I asked her, "Do you see a house in the field behind this house?"

Samantha peered into the distance. "I don't see a house. Is it in the trees?"

"No. I have to tell you something that may convince you I'm psycho."

Samantha laughed until she saw the expression on my face. "You're not joking, are you?"

"Nope."

"Lay your tale on me, and I'll let you know if I think you're psycho."

I told Samantha, but I do not pretend it was an orderly narrative. She listened as my words tumbled into the still air, rotating her gaze between my face and the field, studying both intently.

When I said, "That's about it. You must have tons of questions, so fire away," my panic level was in the stratosphere.

"I believe you," she said quietly. "I don't think you are psycho, weird or delusional. I believe different people see and feel parts of the world around us, but nobody can grasp it all. Sometimes I sense things before they happen, and I often believe I've communicated with mental telepathy.

"Your paranormal ability is nothing to be ashamed of, and you must stop hiding your light under a bushel!"

From that day on, I have done just that.

Samantha and I were married the next year, within two weeks of being graduated from the University of Tennessee. I had a degree in electrical engineering, and landed a job with the National Aeronautics and Space Administration at Cape Canaveral, Florida.

Samantha's degree was in accounting, and she postponed looking for a job until we were settled in a house. Six months later she had a job she liked, and it paid well. A year later, we decided we wanted to have children.

Samantha chose to quit her accounting job and raise the beautiful, healthy twins God gave us. They are grown now, and unless they have kept it secret, neither has any paranormal abilities.

We missed our families, but loved Florida, and we've had a good life here. We've kept in close touch with our families, most of whom still live in Tennessee. We made time for our children to get to know them, and through the years we attended most of the funerals.

My great-great-grandmother, Clementine, died shortly after I asked Samantha to marry me. I felt God had blessed me to let her live until I had another true ally. My grandfather went next, and then my father.

At this point in time my grandmother and mother, and my father's siblings, Callie, Charles and Luther, were all that remained from the older generations that surrounded me as a child.

Funerals always make me reflect about the purpose of my life experiences. After we returned home from my father's funeral, I felt an overwhelming sense that the mystery of my paranormal ability to see the invisible house was about to be revealed to me.

My anxiety level soared. I asked myself if I was going nuts, or what, if anything, I should do to unlock this secret.

The image of the house played constantly in my mind, and this had never happened to me before. To get relief, I sketched the invisible house for the first time in my life. I sent a copy to my grandmother and one to my mother, along with a short note asking them if my sketch looked anything like the house that had stood behind my grandparents' home.

I also asked if there were any pictures of the house. Why I had never asked before, why nobody had shown me a picture, or asked me to sketch the house, I don't know.

A week after I'd posted the letters, my grandmother, Naomi Byrd, called. "Ezekiel, I have your letter. Your sketch is like the house, and I take it as an omen from God Almighty to clear my soul of secrets before I die. You must come to Tennessee as soon as you can so we can talk."

"Granny!"

"It must be just you and me. What I'm going to tell you, I conjured up and carried out. I could do it because I'm a midwife. My intentions were good, but you know the road to Hell is paved with good intentions, and I want God to forgive me for taking on powers that belong only to Him."

Knowing that Granny was never melodramatic, or given to exaggeration, sent waves of pain through me, and my heart was pounding.

"Does my mother know what you're going to tell me?"

"Part of it, yes. Part of it, no. After our talk, you can decide if you want to discuss it with your mother. My advice is not to, but my delusion that I am omnipotent is gone. When can you come to Tennessee?"

"I'll have to make some arrangements, but I can probably leave day after tomorrow. I must tell Samantha I'm going to meet with you in private, and please don't ask me not to tell her whatever it is you're going to tell me."

"I won't. When you come, we can't meet at my house because there's always people in and out. You get a room at the Holiday Inn in Athens, and I'll drive over there."

Within forty-eight hours after Granny's call, I checked into the Holiday Inn. It was raining hard, and I was concerned about Granny driving in it. That proved to be futile, because she pulled in beside me as I was parking in front of my room. I threw her a kiss, and ran to unlock the door.

My golf umbrella was on the back seat, and I got soaked getting it loose from the golf bag. I held it over Granny, and helped her to the door.

Not a word had been spoken. Granny's wrinkled face was tense, and I'm sure mine was even more so. We hugged. Her body felt far more frail than she looked.

"Granny, you've got me on tenterhooks!"

She smiled, and some of the tension went out of her face. "If you can get some ice without getting wetter, please do. We'll need some water while we talk."

I got the ice and my suitcase. While I changed into dry clothes, Granny put two glasses of ice water on the small round table by the window, and pulled up a chair on each side.

Granny asked that I listen closely to her story, and when she'd finished I could ask questions, and then we'd talk. I was relieved that she was composed, and nodded agreement.

This secret rendezvous with Granny lasted about two hours, which I look back upon with a kaleidoscope of emotions and gratitude.

What follows is what I heard on that fateful day.

Granny reminded me that she was a practicing midwife for over forty years, and this profession meant she was with people at very private times in their lives, and she was renowned for keeping their secrets.

In the summer of 1956, a middle-aged woman knocked on her door. A very pretty, and very pregnant, young woman was standing beside her.

"Mrs. Byrd, I'm Connie Clampitt, and this here's my daughter, Evelyn. As you can see, she's about ready to deliver, and your son Charles is the father."

Granny invited them in, because she knew that being married with children had never converted Charles, who is my father's identical twin, to monogamy.

It didn't take long to establish the fact that Charles had dated nineteen-year-old Evelyn the previous winter while he'd been working in Fontana Village, North Carolina. Mrs. Clampitt told Granny that she had learned that Charles was married, but being a devout Christian woman with no desire to break up a home was why she came to her.

She had high hopes for Evelyn, and did not want her to keep the baby. Would Granny deliver the baby and find it a home?

Granny, with tears brimming in her eyes, said, "Ezekiel, at that moment I felt God had answered my prayers for your parents to have a baby. Instantly, a perfect plan was in my mind.

"I told Mrs. Clampitt we could work something out if she and Evelyn would swear to take the secrets of this birth to their grave. They agreed, and so far they have.

"I had no qualms about Mrs. Clampitt, but had lots of them about Evelyn. It turned out she was madly in love with a soldier who was in Vietnam, and they planned to marry. She'd not told him she was pregnant, it would all be done before he got home, and he'd never know.

"Charles and your father had left the previous week to work for a contractor in South Vietnam. They had signed a contract to stay a full year. If they fulfilled that contract, they'd get a big bonus, so barring a calamity they'd be out of the picture for almost a year.

"Evelyn swore she hadn't told Charles, and I believed her. I knew that he had two illegitimate children that he'd never acknowledged. As painful as it was, I had accepted the fact that my leopard would never change his spots.

"The local doctors had told your mother that she would never conceive a child. That depressed her, but she had not told your father, and planned to go to a good fertility clinic for more tests while your father was away.

"Evelyn's coloring is about the same as your mother's, and the blood, etc., would be the same as your father's, so I thought God had given me an airtight plan.

"I told Mrs. Clampitt that I would deliver the baby and find it a home. Another omen that this was preordained was that the hired hand's family had moved out of the house behind ours the previous week.

"Before they left, we agreed that Mrs. Clampitt and Evelyn would move into the house the next week and live there until the baby was born, and Evelyn was well enough to go home. I gave her a check to cover her expenses and help seal their vows of silence.

"I told her I could tell if Charles was the father of Evelyn's baby, and if I was sure he was, I would pay her two thousand dollars. Even if your mother rejected my plan, I knew several other couples who would adopt the baby.

"By now, dear Ezekiel, you know you are that baby. The moment I delivered you, I knew you were Charles' son. You were the spittin' image of him and Caleb the day they were laid in my arms.

"Your mother had accepted my plan with a great sense of relief. She dreaded going to the doctors for tests, since the doctors had been so positive she'd never get pregnant. She wrote the glad tidings to your father. He was ecstatic. She padded herself as the months went along, and nobody suspected.

"The only fly in the ointment was your birth certificate, but since I had the responsibility to register births, I entered a date when your mother would have likely given birth.

"We both knew that this would make you about eight months older than the date on your birth certificate, but that seemed insignificant at the time. You now know why you were always so advanced for your age.

"Evelyn went into labor on July 4, 1956, and as agreed she never saw you, and she has never contacted me. I hope you will not condemn or hate her. Remember, she was a nineteen-year-old kid that Charles took advantage of. When I made this pact with Evelyn and her mother, there was no mention that I would never contact them, but it was implied. I can't control what you do, but if you find her you might disrupt her life.

"As anti-climactic as it may seem, Ezekiel, you know the rest of the story to this point in time. What happens next is up to you."

Granny was exhausted. Every muscle in my body was as tight as a fiddle string, and my brain was too numb for questions.

"Let's go get something to eat, Granny, while I let this sink in. There's a restaurant here in the motel."

"Good. I'm famished."

We ate in silence for several minutes.

"Ezekiel, are you angry with me?"

"No. Tell me again why you decided to tell me."

"It's that drawing you sent. I'd never connected your claims to see a house behind my house with your birth, but when I got your sketch, I knew God had given you the power to see that house, and it was a command from Him that I tell you the truth."

"Do you have any pictures of the house?"

"No. I looked through all my pictures and found lots of pictures of our house, but all of them were taken from the front, and since the house that burned was almost directly behind our house, it could not be seen.

"I remembered that Callie had brought a Navy friend home with her one summer, and he had painted several pictures around the farm. I called Callie, and she found one that shows both houses. It's on the back seat in my car. If you'd like to see it now, here are the keys. Please get it."

I gazed transfixed at the painting. Here, on canvas, was the house behind Granny's house where I'd hidden during games of hide and seek. The house where I'd really been born. I'd always been told I had been born "at home," and "home" was my parents' house. I'd read some weird stories about people who profess to remember things before they are born. Maybe I was one of those weird ones.

Granny said gently, "Now that you know your connection with the house, it may be that you'll never see it again."

"It doesn't matter. I came to terms with it long ago."

"My darling grandson, my confession has laid another heavy load on you, with which you must come to terms."

"Yeah, Granny. This morning in my world, Charles Byrd was my uncle; this afternoon he's my father. Caleb Byrd was my father; this afternoon he's my uncle. Myssi Byrd was my biological mother; this afternoon, she's my adoptive mother. Do you think Charles or Caleb ever suspected?"

"Absolutely not."

"Does Mother think my sketch is a command from God to tell me the truth?"

"No. Her only comment was that you just can't let go of the invisible house."

"I know. It is the only barrier between us."

"She said she'd contact you in a few days, and tell you what she thinks."

"I dread that contact."

"The Serenity Prayer will come in handy here. Remember? "God grant me the serenity to accept the things I cannot change, the courage to change the things I can, and the wisdom to know the difference.""

Granny and I parted about four o'clock. The rain had stopped. We were both tired, but she seemed capable of driving home. After her call that she'd arrived safely, I went for a ride. I rolled the window down, hoping the fresh air would blow away the uninvited medley of emotions that burned in every cell of my body. It would take something stronger than wind through a car window to put out the fire.

By the time I arrived home the next day, I had decided to defer telling anyone what Granny had told me until I was emotionally grounded with the way my life had been recast. I was in the same body, but my psyche was undergoing a major renovation.

I called Granny and told her that her confession was safe with me until she, Charles and Mother were gone, and in case they outlived me, it would be safe for eternity.

Granny had told me about an offer she'd received from a big developer for her part of the farm, and this was enough to satisfy Samantha's curiosity for now.

When my mother called, she said my sketch looked like the house that had burned, and that she did not have any pictures of it. I sensed the same discomfort she'd always displayed about the invisible house, and dropped it.

Life went on, and Granny went to her reward. As far as I know, Charles died without knowing he was my father, and my mother died without knowing that I knew she was not my biological mother. Perhaps she'd have been comforted to know that I've never felt the slightest yearning to find my biological mother.

After Granny, Charles and Mother died, I told my children, and other members of the family, the whole story. They took it in stride, just as they had about my seeing the invisible house.

In this day and age such secrets are the stuff of top television ratings and best-seller books. Several people have suggested that I explore these options. I've found it therapeutic to share my experiences with those who have paranormal abilities, or an interest in the subject.

I still see the house on Old Smoky. Maybe I have the answer to "why," but there may be more.

If I go to the same place the biblical Ezekiel went, I'll ask his opinion.

Chapter 8
A Cow Named Martha

The morning of June 19, 1956, was warm and cloudless. Dr. Phillip Glick was driving his new, bright blue Chevrolet pickup on a winding dirt road about five miles south of Bryson City, North Carolina. He loved the muted melody of birds and leaves swaying in the gentle breeze.

He was driving slow enough to avoid the deep ruts, savor the scenery, and spot ripe blackberries. A couple of times, the vines had been so close to the road that he could pick them without getting out of his truck.

This outing, and the two weeks he'd been here on vacation, had been as therapeutic as Phillip had hoped. This time next week he'd be back on duty in the hospital in Tampa, Florida, trying to help men and women make sense of the contradictions in their topsy-turvy worlds.

Phillip planned to retire next year, and had bought a small farm close to Bryson City, with a house suitable for a married couple, and occasional guests. Although he'd been a widower for almost ten years, and doubted he'd ever marry again, he was ready if the right woman came along.

The house had a cellar, and he was stocking it with wines he made from formulas he'd collected from local folks. This afternoon he'd start a batch of blackberry wine.

He'd filled his last bucket to the brim and was getting into his pickup, when he heard the unmistakable sounds of a cow bawling her head off. The cow was nowhere in sight, but the sounds were ahead. As he rounded the second curve, she was standing halfway between the main road and a side road that led down a rolling hill. No house was in sight, but there was a rickety mailbox at the intersection.

One glance told Phillip that this cow was in great distress. Her distended udder caused her to stand spraddle-legged. Small streams of milk squirted from the teats, and the bell around her neck clanged like claps of thunder as she swung her body in agonized bawling.

He pulled the pickup to the side of the road, got out, and walked toward the cow. Much to his surprise, she took a couple of steps toward him, then stopped and glared at him as if trying to tell him about her plight.

Extending his hand, Phillip said softly, "Easy, old girl. I see you left tracks coming up this side road, so let's go back and get you some help."

The cow continued to bawl pitifully, but allowed Phillip to take hold of the strap that held the bell around her neck.

He rubbed her head, "You've got to get out of the road. This is not India, it's Swain County."

He tugged on the strap, and she allowed him to guide her down the side road. Trees and weeds encroached on the road from both sides, but Phillip caught glimpses of a split rail fence running parallel to the road on the right side. As they rounded the first turn, he could see a small, unpainted, old-fashioned farmhouse, with a barn in back.

It took about five minutes to reach the front yard. "Anybody here?" Dead silence. Not even a watchdog.

The cow reduced her bawling to a low moan, and headed toward the open gate to the barnyard. Phillip stepped up his pace, went through the gate on the cow's heels, and closed it. The metal-barred gate moved on well-oiled hinges, in sharp contrast to the rickety mailbox at the end of the road.

When he turned, the cow was standing about twenty feet away, looking down into the small creek that ran past the barn. She swung her head wildly and bawled with all her might. "Good God!" Phillip shouted. "You're trying to tell me something! What is it, old girl?"

The moment he started toward her, Phillip heard a faint female voice: "Help! I'm down in the creek!" Adrenaline propelled him to the cow's side, and he saw a woman in the creek. Her shoulders were against the bank, and water was trickling over most of her body from her waist to her toes.

The woman called out again. "I'm close to the cow. Help!"

"I see you! Hold on. I'll get you out."

Phillip slid down the steep five-foot bank, then stood up in front of her. The water was clear and surprising cold.

The woman appeared to be about sixty, slim, with a deep tan, and short gray hair. She wore overalls, a flannel shirt with long sleeves, and rubber boots. There was no blood or visible injuries.

"Thank God for sending you!" she yelled.

"I see your feet are wedged between two rocks. Do you think you have any broken bones?"

"Don't think so. I'm cold, but I'm not in pain. I can wiggle my toes, and I can move my head and arms."

"Good. I'll move one of these rocks, and you pull your legs toward you as quick as you can."

"Okay."

Phillip grasped the smaller of the two rocks that were wedging her feet and tried to rotate it. After a few heaves, it slipped slightly, and the woman jerked her feet free.

"You're agile! Give me your hands, and I'll pull you up. If you feel pain, stop," he commanded firmly.

The woman nodded. Her grasp was strong, and within a few seconds she was on her feet. She swayed slightly. The cow stopped bawling and watched silently.

"I'm a bit blind and dizzy."

"Normal. Hold on to my hands, and stand a minute or two. When you feel able, we'll walk down to that spot where it looks like we can step out of the creek.

"We can. I'm Lucy Winters. Thank you for saving my life. If you hadn't come along chances are I'd be the late Lucy Winters."

"I'm Phillip Glick. I'm on vacation and was picking blackberries up on the main road. Your cow was up there, bawling her head off. We'll talk details when we get you in the house and make sure you're okay. I'm a doctor, so I can check you if you wish. My truck is parked up on the road, and if you prefer, I will take you to your doctor."

"God did send a well-qualified good samaritan!"

Phillip examined Lucy. She was tired, cold, and had bruises on most of her body, but was not suffering from hypothermia. While she was getting into warm clothes, Phillip heated a can of soup and made coffee.

"This hot stuff will help you get warm."

"Thanks. Soup and coffee never smelled so good. I'm dying to know about you and Martha."

"Martha?"

"My cow. Her name is Martha. She needs milking, but I'm not up to it just yet. That's what I was on my way to do when I got wedged in the creek."

"How did it happen?"

"We had a heavy rain last week. Lots of small trees fell

from the banks and made dams in the creek. I always clear them because they hold silt and will clog the creek."

"I usually walk in the creek, throw them out, drag them outside the fence, then burn them after they dry. I saw a big one near the footbridge, so I left the gate open to get it out. I stood at the rim, leaned forward, and pulled hard. It came out, and I went in!

"I heard Martha's bell when she left and that gave me hope that somebody would bring her back. Thank God that's what happened. I don't know if she went for help or just happened to wander to the right place at the right time, but thank you for coming to our rescue.

"While I was lying there, I alternated between thinking about dying and trying to get my feet loose. It was a puzzle, how my feet were small enough to slip between those rocks, but too big to pull out."

"Surely you didn't expect to die," Phillip said incredulously. "Didn't you expect someone to come along?"

"You've been too polite to pry, but I live alone. Just Martha and me. My neighbors on either side are both about a mile away, and I seldom see them.

"A great-aunt willed me this place a couple of years ago. At that time I was married, living in town — Bryson City — and teaching my last year of fifth grade before retirement. Since then, I have retired, my husband died and left me with huge medical bills. I sold my house in town and moved here to make ends meet."

"You're a brave woman."

"Thanks for saying that, but I just did what I had to do. I'm feeling better, but can I impose on you to milk Martha?"

"Milking is not on my skills list, but I'll give it a try. When I was a kid, I milked my grandparents' cow once or twice. I didn't take to it, because Grandma made me put on her apron because her cows weren't used to being milked by menfolks. I liked to hunt the cows and hear the whip-poorwills calling."

Martha saw Phillip coming and greeted him with a friendly moo. He patted her head, sat down on the milking stool, and began zigzagging streams of milk into the two-gallon zinc water bucket. It was almost full when Martha's teats ran dry.

"Feel better, Martha? Of course you do. I've seen a lot of cows in my time, but you're the smartest one. When I was a boy, my aunt let me ride her cow. I was in India for many years, and got to know several sacred cows. I'm glad we met, and that your intelligence saved Lucy's life."

"You're a fine human being, Phillip Glick," Lucy declared as she walked toward him.

Phillip picked up the milk bucket and turned around. He felt a bit abashed at Lucy's having heard him conversing with Martha, until he saw she had tears in her eyes.

"Lucy, I really did ride a cow, and I have a picture to prove it. I went to India shortly after I completed my internship, and worked for five years in an American missionary hospital. I got to know a lot about their sacred cows."

Lucy embraced Martha's head, and patted her gently. "You'd probably have gone on your way without telling me, but I'm glad I heard you tell Martha.

"She's an intelligent cow. I love her for companionship, as well as the sustenance she provides. I'm going to pray to the power that created her to grant me some insight into what happened today. I guess it could be called a miracle."

"I won't argue."

"You must show me the picture of you riding a cow," Lucy said with a impish grin.

"I'll bring you a copy of the picture, and a bottle of blackberry wine from the berries I picked today."

Chapter 9
Ghost Mystery Solved

Charles Delozier herded his Southern Railway train around the tracks between Judson and Bryson City, North Carolina, for seventeen years. Judson was a small community of approximately 600 people. It went to a watery grave in 1944 when Fontana Dam was completed and the lake began to fill. Bryson City is still alive and well.

For many years the train made two trips a day, hauling passengers and freight. The railroad had brought a better life to the people who had lived in isolation and poverty. People still waved when the train roared by, and Charles always greeted them with a quick whistle toot.

When he took over the job from Jack Ledbetter, he was required to make a week's runs under his watchful eye. On the second day, a misty rain made the tracks slick, and this meant driving at a lower speed and using the headlight.

About ten minutes out of Bryson City, Charles saw a tall man in overalls standing beside the tracks who seemed poised to hop on the train. Charles blew the whistle, and Jack Ledbetter broke into a hearty belly laugh. Charles looked at him, but neither one attempted to talk over the roar of the train.

When they pulled into the Southern depot in Judson,

Charles asked for an explanation.

Jack grinned like a man with infinite wisdom tolerating the uninformed. "I'll bet my last chew of tobacco that you saw a man, and you tooted the whistle because you thought he was going to jump on the train."

"Yeah, but what's so funny about that?"

"Son, you saw a ghost. He's been there for a couple of years. At first I thought I was seeing a reflection of the light on the bushes or something, but when I saw him on clear days, I was really bumfuzzled. I asked around, and some of the hands and some of the passengers had seen him. Common sense told me that no man's going to be there as many times as I've seen him. I don't cotton to the notion of ghosts, but this has made a believer out of me."

Charles had great respect for Jack Ledbetter, and he did not believe he was joshing him or making up a tale. "Do you know who it could be? Did anybody get killed trying to hop the train there?"

Jack shook his head. "I don't think so. A couple of drunks got killed, but they were on the trestle. If anybody got killed there, nobody blamed the railroad."

"Have you ever stopped when you see him?"

"No, but I've slowed way down many a time, and he's gone in a flash, just like today."

"I'm thankful that I saw him while you're still on the job. If there's a ghost on that run, he ain't hurt you, so it stands to reason he won't hurt me, but if you hadn't told me what you think, it might have preyed on my mind and caused me to wreck the train. I'm obliged to you, Jack."

"I ain't talked this around the bosses."

"I get your drift."

Jack had been telling the truth. The man was there more times than not, rain or shine. Crew members and regular passengers reported seeing him. By the end of Charles' second year on the run, he had dubbed the "ghost" the "hobo," because he was still hoping for an explanation of the man he saw.

As bitter a pill as it was for Charles to swallow, he could find nothing to explain the hobo except that he was a ghost. He'd talked to a lot of people who firmly believed in ghosts, and their theory was that ghosts were the spirits of people who had once lived. That being the case, Charles reasoned, the ghost had a name when he was alive.

The ghost believers, and a couple of books Charles read about researching ghosts, indicated that ghosts were apt to stay around the place where they drew their last breath.

The next logical step seemed to be to find out if any man had died at that spot. Jack had said only that if anybody had died there, the railroad had not been blamed.

Charles asked around among crew members and passengers, and got his first clue. Edith Smiley was a regular passenger, and she lived about a mile from the hobo's haunt. Charles asked her if anyone had been killed there.

"They've found three dead men around there in the last few years. Two were the Gibby boys. They were drunk as skunks and got run over on the trestle. About a year after that another man was found dead on the tracks, but it was somebody who hadn't lived here very long. Since he didn't have family, we never got the straight of it."

"Do you know who found him?"

"No, but whoever it was called the Swain County sheriff."

It hadn't occurred to Charles to go to the sheriff. People in these parts buried their own dead.

Joshua Hite had been sheriff for about ten years, and Charles knew him well.

"I'm here to inquire about a man who was found dead

on the railroad tracks between here and Judson some time back. I've been told you were called. What can you tell me?"

"Yeah, I was called. Jeb Riley found him. He was stretched out face down between the rails. The train had run over him, but he was not mangled up. Jeb knows most everybody in the county, but he'd never seen that dead man, so he sent for me. I called Doc Bacon and a couple of deputies, and we rode over to take a look.

"There were no signs of injury, even after the deputies turned him face up. His eyes were wide open, and the weirdest set of eyes I've ever seen. One was blue, the other jet black.

"Doc cocked his red head to one side and said, 'Looks like jimson weed poison killed him. Let's get him off the tracks so you can look in his pockets to see if there's anything to tell us who he is.'

"I went through his pockets. The only thing that gave us a clue who he might be was a letter in the bib pocket of his overalls. It had been mailed to: Luther Evins, Route 3, Pikeville, Tennessee. The sender turned out to be Rena Campbell, and I knew she lived within a mile. I sent the deputies to fetch her."

As Josh talked, Charles recalled hearing that a man had been poisoned to death, but he didn't recall hearing he'd been found on the railroad tracks. "Did he turn out to be Luther Evins?"

"Yeah. Rena Campbell identified him. He'd come over

from Pikeville the previous summer to stay with an aunt and uncle while he looked for work. They live up the hill from Rena. I'd read the letter, and told Rena I had, so she might as well come clean about her and Evins. Rena's a hard-up grass widow.

"While Evins was here looking for work last summer, he and Rena got together. For some reason he went back to Pikeville, and Rena had written him to come back because she missed him. He'd been back about a month before we found him dead. Rena found out he'd been riding the train down to Judson to see another woman, and she raised hell.

"Doc determined that he was poisoned with jimson weed. It was in his blood, and had also been put in one eye. That's why it was jet black."

Charles was astonished. "You mean jimson weed makes eyes turn black? Never heard that."

"It does, but only temporarily. How long it lasts depends on how much is put in the eye. Neither Doc or I thought he put the weed in his eye, or took enough of the stuff to kill him. Rena's tale was that he made tea and smoked jimson weed leaves because he liked the way it made him feel.

"Doc said it produces hallucinations, and in Evins' case he died from cardiovascular collapse, which means a heart attack. Rena admitted she was jealous, but denied she had poisoned him. I poked around, but came up dry. His uncle buried him in the family plot next to his house. What's your interest in this?"

Charles summarized why he had inquired. To his relief, Josh did not laugh, so he concluded his summary by asking, "Have you ever seen this ghost or heard this ghost tale?"

"No, I've never seen him, but I've heard about the railroad ghost plenty of times. I thought it was just another ghost tale. Don't be hesitant about telling folks you've seen him, because half the people in this county see ghosts, and love to talk about it."

Charles thanked Josh, and went straight to Jack Ledbetter's house to tell him the news. Jack listened with an amused grin until Charles finished.

"Well, son, you put a name to the ghost. That solves the mystery of who he is, but do you think he'll go away now?"

Charles shook his head. "I doubt it, but I'll not be seeing him much longer. Word's out that they are going to start filling Fontana Dam next year, and that means the train run between Bryson and Judson will end. When the tracks go under water, maybe he'll stop trying to hop the train."

Chapter 10
Footlog Phantom

Cleve Davis's doney-gal, Lola Lambert, lived on one side of Forney Creek, and he lived on the other. In 1907, doney-gal was the term young men in his family used when they talked about their very special sweethearts.

Forney Creek was a sparsely settled wilderness, and sometimes folks learned they had a new neighbor by seeing the smoke from a new cabin. This is how Cleve found Lola.

He'd been hunting up on a ridge behind their log cabin, and saw smoke coming from the other side of the creek. That night at supper, he told his pa he was sure he'd seen smoke from a chimney, not a campfire, and thought it was a good idea to go over and take a look. His three younger brothers chimed in, eager to go.

His pa agreed, as mountaineers were always eager for news to break the drab monotony of their isolated lives, but ruled one was enough to take a look, and since Cleve had spotted the smoke he'd know where to go.

The only way to "go over and take a look" was to walk. The Davis family had a milk cow, and two oxen for plowing and pulling their sled.

Cleve crossed Forney Creek early next morning by hopping from rock to rock. There was a footlog about a quarter mile down the creek, but he used it only when the water was high on the rocks.

Photograph courtesy of Richard Weisser and smokyphotos.com

It was a fine morning in April, and going to take a look for a new cabin sure beat grubbing tree roots out of hard and rocky soil to make "new ground" for planting corn. The smoke might turn out to be moonshiners, so he'd be cautious.

Cleve followed an old trail that his uncle had hacked through these acres when he was still hopeful of finding copper or some other mineral to mine. The mark on one of the giant oak trees told him he'd walked half a mile from the creek.

When he turned his attention back to the trail, he stopped dead in his tracks. A beautiful girl was coming toward him, staring with wide-eyed amazement. Every hormone in his nineteen-year-old body came alive.

She stopped. "Howdy. Where you headed?"

The smile on her face was the sweetest Cleve had ever seen. He stammered, "I live on yon side of the creek, and yesterday I saw chimney smoke. I'm looking to see if there's a new cabin. Forney's building up fast these days."

"Must have seen smoke from our cabin. Pa and my brothers worked on it all winter. We come from Kentucky last summer, and been staying with Pa's sister. She wrote to Pa that a man was going to start a sawmill close by and he hopes to get on at it."

"Yeah, we heard talk of that too, and I'd like to try my hand at it. Where're you going?"

"Down to the creek to fish a spell. I left my pole, and hoe I dig worms with, down there. If you want to see our cabin, I'll walk back with you. If I don't Papa will ask if you saw me. He likes to know who's about, but he don't get on the other side of the creek much."

They had walked less than five minutes when a new clearing on the hillside, with a cabin in the middle of it, came into view. There was no smoke from the chimney. Three men were nailing wooden shingles on the roof.

An older man called out, "Lola, that's a mighty big fish you caught."

Cleve saw that he was grinning, and dropped his caution.

Lola giggled. "He's from across the creek, Pa. Seen our smoke, and his pa sent him to find out if they have new neighbors."

Lola's pa said, "You can tell him Tom Lambert and his family are his new neighbors. What's your name, and who's your pa?"

"Cleve Davis. My pa's Elwood. Lived around here all his life."

"My sister Vernie married a local and moved here from Kentucky. She knows your pa, and told Lola he had some big strapping boys. She's been going down to the creek hoping to see for herself, and today she found one."

Cleve's face turned crimson, and sweat covered his brow. He'd never heard such plain talk, but he seized the moment. "I'm the oldest, and I'd like to come court Lola." He glanced at her. She turned her eyes away, but a broad smile lingered.

"Sounds suitable, but courtin' it'd better be. No more 'til you make an honest woman of her."

Cleve skipped back across the rocks, and into the kitchen where his mother, Mamie, was cooking the noon meal. Before he could speak, she observed, "You're mighty feisty!"

"I found the new cabin. Tom Lambert and his family are our new neighbors."

Mamie grinned at her first-born son. "Now I know why you're so feisty. Tom's got a daughter about your age."

"Yeah, he has. How'd you know?"

"I was young once."

"Her name is Lola, and she's just turned sixteen, and mighty pretty. She was going to the creek to fish, and I met her on the trail, so she went back to the cabin with me.

"Her pa and two of her brothers were shingling the roof. I reckoned Lola hadn't been gone long enough for him to think we'd been up to no good. He said he'd stop by the first time he's on this side of the creek and say howdy."

That summer Cleve and Lola spent every moment they could escape from their chores together. They'd meet at the footlog, because Lola was timid about hopping from rock to rock to cross the creek.

It was a three-mile walk from the footlog to the nearest church, and they became regular attendees.

In late September, it rained hard for a week. The creek rose so high that it covered all the rocks and the footlog. Lola would stand on her side of the creek, Cleve on his, and wave. The rushing water, filled with uprooted trees, made it impossible to yell back and forth.

When the water level fell, Lola and Cleve rushed across the footlog to meet each other. Cleve lost his footing and fell into the raging creek. His body was found a few days later, and he was buried on his family's homestead.

Lola was inconsolable, and swore that the devil had

greased the footlog. One evening, she was sitting on the creek bank, trying to pray like the preacher had told her to do to get over her grief, when she saw Cleve on the footlog. She jumped up and ran toward him, but he vanished.

Lola had been taught that believing in ghosts was a sin. She told no one she'd seen Cleve's ghost, but a short time later, several people told her they'd seen him on the footlog. Before long it was the talk of the community, and people began to refer to Cleve as "the footlog phantom."

This love story has been passed from generation to generation, and become a local legend.

Author's Note: Forney Creek is one of the tributaries that flows into Fontana Lake in western North Carolina. Visitors to this area can enjoy many coves along Forney Creek as it rises and falls with the lake's demand for water, and who knows — you might see Cleve!

Photograph by Juanitta Baldwin

Chapter 11
Merlin — Magickal Cat

Mandy Tolliver's home is on a small farm, with two barns that are unused, and Nature is recycling them. When she and her husband, Gilbert, were farming, they kept cats in the barns for rat control, but they did not keep a cat in the house. All the cats had names, and an ample diet. Mandy enjoyed watching them romp, and marveled at how they sat on the fence and watched the moon.

She'd heard dozens of superstitions about cats all her life, but she'd never heard of cat magick until she visited a museum in Egypt. There she learned that the Egyptians used two basic forms of cat magick: one to benefit humans, dead or alive, and one to bring harm to others.

This new information explained something weird that had happened with her grandson, Jimmy, and his cat, Merlin. At the time of the weird happening Jimmy was the only one in the family who had a cat.

He lived with his parents, Mandy's son, Seth, and daughter-in-law, Lorene, in a house close by. He is their only child and loves animals. He cajoled his parents to let him add a cat to his menagerie of a dog, hamster, and rooster. On his twelfth birthday they relented, and allowed him to pick a cat from an accommodating neighbor's litter.

The first afternoon after Jimmy got his kitten, he brought it to meet Mandy, announcing proudly that he had named it Merlin because he'd read some stories about cats doing magic tricks.

In midafternoon a couple of weeks later, Jimmy, Merlin and his dog, Champ, walked over to Mandy's house. Mandy and Jimmy enjoyed lemonade, and she made points with Jimmy by having dog and cat treats.

When they started home, Mandy saw Merlin go to the base of a cherry tree and begin digging furiously. Jimmy laughed and ran back to tell Mandy that Merlin was digging for buried treasure. Mandy walked to the tree and jokingly agreed that maybe some of the rumors of buried treasure were true.

When Jimmy was ready to go, Merlin was not, and he did not follow Jimmy when he and Champ walked away. Jimmy came back and reached down to pick Merlin up. Merlin skirted around the tree two or three times before Jimmy got a firm grasp on him. He did not scratch, but was very vocal.

Every time Jimmy brought Merlin to Mandy's house, he'd run to the cherry tree and dig, then protest when the time came to leave. When Merlin was about six months old, he was allowed to go out on his own. He'd make a beeline to the cherry tree, and gradually developed a routine of digging for a while, then sitting on the dirt he'd scratched up. He'd sit absolutely still and stare at the ground for varying lengths of time. This would go on for a couple of hours when Jimmy was at home, and much longer when Jimmy was in school. He seemed to know the time, and usually trotted home by the time the school bus was due.

Mandy thought Merlin's behavior was strange, but since it was harmless she thought little about it until the cherry tree was ringed with holes. What, she wondered occasionally, drew him to the tree like a magnet? There were no signs of moles. There were some red worms, but he never showed any interest in eating them. When he was in his staring cycle, he was not distracted by the insects and birds that flew all around his circle of vision.

When school was out, Jimmy asked Mandy if he could dig up the cherry tree, because he was sure Merlin knew there was something buried there. He said he wanted to do this because when he went back to school they always had to write about what they'd done during the summer, and nobody else would have a story about digging up a tree, and he'd have a super story if he found a buried treasure.

Since this was one of a dozen or so cherry trees, Mandy said okay. Jimmy and Merlin spent many hours digging. Seth liked to spend time with his son, so he'd stop by once in a while to talk and dig a bit.

After digging a complete circle around the tree, they'd found nothing but soil, a few small rocks and red worms.

Mandy supplied lemonade, and often made pictures. One hot afternoon, Merlin lay down about six feet from the tree trunk at the deepest part that had been dug. When Jimmy stopped for lemonade, Merlin did not follow him to the porch for his treat. Jimmy took him his treat and tried to pick him up, but he made it clear he wanted to stay put, so Jimmy returned to the porch

When he came back, he nudged Merlin and began digging where he'd been lying. The soil was moist from recent rains, and that made it easier to drive the shovel deeper into the ground. Jimmy had stepped on the shovel with both feet when he felt something solid, and heard a dull thud. Thinking it was probably a rock, he wiggled the shovel to find an edge, but could not. Merlin jumped around in a circle, and Jimmy got excited. He ran to the house and called for Mandy to come. She went with him to the hole as he explained he'd struck something big. Merlin was still jumping around.

Mandy said later that she felt excited and frightened. She got a shovel and helped Jimmy dig. In a few minutes they had uncovered a piece of metal more than a foot square. It seemed to have some type of pattern on it. They were tired, but determined to unearth their find.

After about an hour later of digging gingerly, they could see that the metal was the top of an old-fashioned metal trunk. At this point Mandy wanted help with the dig, be-cause she thought it wise to have other adults present since she could not imagine what they'd find in the trunk.

They suspended operations until Seth and Lorene came home about five o'clock. Jimmy was so afraid someone would see "our buried treasure" that he spread a light cover of dirt over the trunk to protect it while they waited. Merlin lay down on top of it and went to sleep.

Seth and Lorene looked at the trunk top. It seemed solid, but if the trunk sides had rusted it had to be removed very carefully. It was decided to get several people to help. Fortunately this was Friday, so they'd be able to commandeer several cousins and friends for Saturday.

At eleven o'clock on Saturday morning, a strong canvas was inserted under the old rusty trunk and it was lifted onto the grass. It was a little over four feet long and almost three feet high. The top and sides had dried somewhat during the delicate digging operation, but the bottom was damp. The canvas was strung between two trees so the air could circulate around the bottom.

Everybody gathered on the porch to relax, eat, and speculate on who had buried the trunk, when it had been buried, and what was in it.

A car drove up, and a middle-aged woman got out and came to the steps. Glances around told Mandy that no one knew her. Mandy introduced herself and asked if she could help her.

The woman introduced herself as Laurie McDermott, and said she'd come because she'd heard about the trunk, and her father, who was in the car, had told her he knew its history.

Cold shivers raced up and down Mandy's spine. "This is a surprise. Would your father like to take a look at the trunk and tell us what he knows?" she asked.

"Yes, I'll get him. His name is Judson Miller. He's lived in Jackson County all his life, so some of you may know him, or about him, or my brothers. He's 97, but still has his wits about him."

Excitement surged through the group, and they moved

quickly to where the trunk was drying. Some commented that they knew some of the Millers, and a few recognized the man who came through the gate.

He smiled and walked to the trunk without aid. Seth brought him a chair, and after looking at the trunk for a couple of minutes the man sat down and told them what he believed about the trunk in a soft, somewhat halting voice.

"What I am about to tell you I heard many times from my father, and other men who lived during the Civil War. When you open this trunk you'll find bones of an 'outliver.' Most of you don't know what an outliver was, but these mountains were full of them during the Civil War. They were men who did not belong to either the North or the South. They hid out here to stay out of the war. They built crude shacks for shelter. These desperate, hungry men raided homes and farms to survive.

"Since we're close to the state line, outlivers went back and forth between North Carolina and Tennessee to plunder. Confederate troops tried to guard the trails and wagon roads through these mountains. When they could not capture the outlivers they shot them down, so by the end of the war most of them just stayed in one state or the other.

"It got so bad here that the men of the area banded together and lay in wait for them. Ten outlivers were sneaking beside this road, and they shot all of them to death. They buried all of them in a common grave except one young man. The man who lived on this place, in a house that is no longer here, was so moved at the sight of the young man, about the age of his son who had been killed in the war, that he buried him in a trunk. It's got to be this one."

A week later, the local sheriff pried the trunk open, found bones just as Mr. Miller had said, and took it away.

Jimmy was disappointed that the trunk was not full of buried treasure, but since the story made the national news, he had his super story for school.

Merlin never goes where the trunk was buried. Mandy thinks it's because he completed his mission.

Chapter 12
Ghost or UFO?

The teller of this story requested anonymity as a condition of telling it to me, because if his neighbors or customers knew about his experience they might suspect he no longer has both oars in the water. I chose Daniel Kirk as a *nom de plume*, and he said that was acceptable.

I met Daniel Kirk in Pigeon Forge, Tennessee, in January 2002 during Wilderness Wildlife Week. For the past fifteen years, the city of Pigeon Forge has hosted this event. Experts on nature and the great outdoors host walks, hikes, seminars and lectures on a wide variety of topics, including Smoky Mountain history and plant and animal life.

I was sharing some of the stories from my books *Smoky Mountain Mysteries* and *Unsolved Disappearances in the Great Smoky Mountains* with a group of almost two hundred people. During the question-and-answer session Daniel Kirk stood and said, "I'm not given to fanciful stories or far-out theories, but some people think that UFOs abduct people. During your research for the unsolved disappearances book, did this possibility come up?"

"Yes, it did," I replied. "I interviewed several people who had been with the people shortly before they disappeared. None of them reported anything to give credence to this possibility. However, several people I interviewed who helped search for the missing people did raise the UFO possibility. It comes up at many discussions, such as we're having here. Real or not, unidentified flying objects, UFOs, have become a permanent part of civilized life on planet Earth."

After the session ended, Daniel Kirk told me this story, which was the basis for his question about UFOs.

On Thanksgiving Day weekend in 1994, Daniel Kirk, and two friends from Nevada hiked from the Clingmans Dome parking lot to Gregory Bald. They arrived at the Bald, which is nearly 5,000 feet above sea level, about two o'clock in the afternoon. The day was exceptionally clear so they had a good view of Parsons Bald to the west and Cheoah Bald to the south.

While they rested and ate, they speculated about the mystery of the "balds." The balds are mountain tops, scattered throughout western North Carolina and east Tennessee at varying altitudes, that refuse to support the growth of trees. Why this is so continues to be a botanical mystery, in spite of several rather convincing theories that have been advanced in recent years.

Kirk told his friends the Cherokee Indian legend of Gregory Bald. Their name for it is "Tsistuyi," which means "the rabbit place." According to their legend, multitudes of rabbits constructed fine "town houses" on the bald and lived there in peace and security under their leader, the

Great Rabbit, who was as large as a deer.

The trio split up shortly after three o'clock to explore and photograph the bald, and agreed to meet back at the spot where they'd rested no later than four-thirty so they would be back at the Clingmans Dome parking lot before dark.

Gregory Bald, like all other balds, has a gently sloping top, not steep or rugged. Kirk made his way to the edge of the bald, hoping to locate a strong flowing spring that a friend had reported finding on the south side of the bald during a previous hike.

He walked toward the tree line and turned east around the perimeter of the bald, listening for the sound of running water. Instead of running water, he heard something crashing in the trees below the bald. Thinking it was a bear, he stopped and peered into the trees.

A transparent sphere, about the length of an old Beetle Volkswagen, floated across his line of sight. It touched the ground, and a bright light inside the sphere switched off and on a few times. It illuminated the sphere, and Kirk thought he saw two human-shaped figures inside.

He said he was momentarily stunned, but kept his eyes riveted on the sphere. A tremendous flow of disconnected impressions washed over him. To steady himself, he backed up against a tree. The standoff began to take on a dreamlike quality.

He stood motionless as the sphere floated away, but

jumped out of his dreamlike state when he heard another crash in the trees. Although it seemed like hours, Kirk's watch told him the incident had ended in about two minutes. Regaining his equilibrium, he was tempted to go look for a crash, but common sense carried the day.

He scrambled to get back to his friends, and asked them if they'd seen anything unusual. Both said they'd seen a strange light, but neither had seen a sphere or heard a crash.

Kirk told them what he'd experienced, and was disappointed that they could not confirm the most spectacular part of his story, but they believed him.

On the hike up, they had met several hikers going down, but had seen no one on the bald. They debated about doing a search, but realized it was foolhardy to begin a search so late in the day without any equipment.

In the cold light of the next day, Kirk said he abandoned all thoughts of searching for the sphere. He knows he saw, and felt, something abnormal. What it was, he will probably never know, but he no longer scoffs at others who report seeing UFOs and ghosts.

He concluded by observing, "Nobody has figured out why the balds are in the mountains. They may be UFO landing sites, and what I saw was a UFO or the ghost of one that crashed!"

Chapter 13
Phantom Mule Team

Toot Hollow is in the foothills of the Great Smoky Mountains in western North Carolina. In 1935, Frank Swain was "churched" from the Toot Hollow Baptist Church for lying about whipping his mule team.

Jule Loveday and Ashe Thorn, movers and shakers in the church, brought the charges. Jule swore before the congregation, with his hand on the Bible, that on Wednesday he'd been walking on the right side of the road that runs by the church and had to jump down the bank to keep from being run over by Frank Swain's wagon.

"Frank was standing up in the wagon, whipping his two mules like no Christian would ever do. The poor dumb pitiful creatures were running for their lives," Jule declared.

Ashe swore, also with his hand on the Bible, that he'd come along in his car just as Jule was climbing up the bank. "Brother Jule ain't as young as he used to be, and except for the Almighty he'd be in the graveyard. He told me what happened, and we went and talked to Frank. He looked us square in the eyes, and lied by denying that he'd whipped his mules, just controlled them with light snaps of the whip.

"Brother Jule and me have followed Scripture. We got some of the church brethren to go with us to talk to Frank, hoping he'd repent. He has not repented one iota. He's here today, so, preacher, we turn it over to you."

The preacher denounced the sin of lying at the top of his voice until he worked the congregation into the ecstasy that most mountain people in that day and age loved.

"Save yourself, Brother Frank — repent! Repent ye of your sins, and go do good work, fer if ye don't, on Judgment Day God Almighty will hurl ye into the fires of hell. Repent, brother!"

Frank Swain shared with his fellow mountaineers an amazing fondness for theological dispute. He'd been known to be whetted to a fighting edge over what a passage of biblical text really meant, and could hold his own with any preacher. He stood and walked to the front of the church and planted his feet firmly on the side reserved for men. In those days, men sat on one side of the church, women on the other.

Glaring at Jule and Ashe with cold steely eyes, Frank Swain said, "Preacher, Jule is lying about me whipping my mules. I didn't do it, so I have nothing to lie about.

"Preacher, you must read a different Bible than I do. My Bible tells me salvation is by faith alone, not by works. I know I have faith. So church away! It won't mean a thing on Judgment Day!"

Such defiance was unexpected, and the perplexed preacher suggested that the charges be "tabled" until the next Sunday.

"No!" Frank yelled. "Do the deed, and answer for it!"

After an hour of prayer and argument, Frank was churched. He never again set foot in the church, or spoke to Jule or Ashe. They remained in power until they died. Preachers who preached the Word as they understood it stayed, and those that didn't moved on.

Frank died in April about four years after he was churched. Jule and Ashe survived him. In June, Toot Hollow held its annual revival meeting. After the service closed at dusk one night, Jule, Ashe, and several other men and young boys followed their usual custom of congregating in the churchyard to debate some point of dogma or gossip.

Suddenly a command from Jule rang out loud and clear: "Listen! Look up the road! I hear a runaway wagon. Some of you young bucks get ready to tackle the horses."

The crowd obeyed, but within seconds there were soft whispered exchanges that nobody was hearing anything.

Ashe yelled, "Everyone get back from the road! Here it

comes! He's going to split this churchyard wide open!"

The churchyard was in fact split wide open, but only with a roar of hoots, laughter, and gibes at Jule and Ashe. The boldness of the crowd reflected long pent-up grievances against the two men.

They were shaken to the core by the near brush with a runaway mule team that nobody else saw or heard, and the disrespectful behavior of the crowd they deemed to be their subjects.

"Go home, you infidels!" Ashe shouted.

The preacher exhorted everybody to go home and pray. Ashe and Jule were getting on in years, and he feared their minds had snapped. Most left quickly, but those who were driving wagons took time to light their lanterns and exchange quips to watch out for ghosts on the way home.

Jule and Ashe got into Ashe's new Chevrolet and talked it over. They had seen and heard the ghosts of Frank Swain and his mules. God was either punishing them or testing their faith.

The story goes that from that night in June, Jule and Ashe saw and heard Frank Swain's wagon pass by the churchyard at odd times as long as they lived. Just when they thought they'd prayed enough for God to put Frank Swain back into Hell where belonged, here he'd come.

Chapter 14
The Ghost Who Wants to Go Home

Margaret Lambert, a war bride and five months pregnant, arrived in Sevier County, Tennessee, on January 8, 1946. She had married Royce Lambert in her home town of Coventry, England, where he was serving in the U.S. Army during World War II.

Royce was a mechanic, and had worked to ready the equipment for D-Day, but he was not sent into that battle. As soon as the war ended in 1945, Royce made arrangements for his bride to travel to his ancestral home and stay with his family until he returned. He anticipated being discharged in March 1946, and, hopefully, be home in time for planting the tobacco crop.

Margaret had never traveled outside of England until she boarded the ship for America. She had hoped one of Royce's five sisters would meet her when she arrived in New York, but no one did. A military bus took her to the Greyhound bus station, and a soldier helped her buy a ticket for Knoxville, Tennessee.

Forty hours later, about seven o'clock in the morning, she arrived in Knoxville, and called the number Royce had given her. His mother answered, and sounded a bit surprised that she had "got here so soon." She instructed Margaret to stay put, and said somebody would be down about dinner time to pick her up.

Margaret was so exhausted that the prospect of staying in the bus station all day gave her the courage to protest. "I am so tired; can't somebody come by noon?"

"That's what I said — somebody, probably Sue, that's Royce's sister, will be there by dinner time. We always eat our dinner at twelve, but I'll wait today until you get here."

"Thank you. I thought dinner was about seven."

Sue did arrive at ten-thirty, and greeted Margaret politely, but with a pronounced reserve. There was little conversation on the drive to the family farm. Royce had told her they lived about five miles from the nearest neighbor, but she had not comprehended that the home was on a dirt road in the middle of the woods.

Royce's mother, father, and three siblings greeted her with the same polite reserve Margaret had shown. Sue showed her to the room "we've fixed for you until Royce gets a place," and asked her to come to the dining room quickly because dinner was late. It was twelve-fifteen.

The cultural shock, and being pregnant among strangers, compounded Margaret's homesickness. She tried not to whine, but cried buckets in private. When she learned that Royce's mother had arranged for a midwife to deliver her baby, she was too depressed to protest.

Royce arrived on March 15, and Margaret poured out her heart to him. He listened, but seemed genuinely puzzled by some of the things she said were troubling her.

He sympathized somewhat with some of the language difficulties she was experiencing, but reminded her he'd run into that with *her* family. He promised to help her overcome her fear of the farm animals and woods. "But why on earth," he asked, "would you not want the best midwife around to deliver our baby?"

The midwife delivered Royce Lambert Jr. on May 1, and shortly thereafter the family moved into a small log house beside the community cemetery. It had running water, electricity, and a wood stove. Royce Jr. was healthy, and Margaret worked diligently at adjusting to her new life.

In June a letter arrived from Anthony Barstow, a first cousin of Margaret, asking if he could come and stay with them for a while. He wanted to move his family to America, and all his papers were in order to leave within a month's time, and he hoped to land a construction job.

Royce was reluctant, but hoping a family member would cheer Margaret up, he agreed. He talked to Lee McAfee, a construction contractor, and he agreed to give Anthony a try.

Anthony Barstow arrived on July 5, and his English accent was like heavenly music to Margaret's ears. He went to work with McAfee, who drove him to and from work.

He helped her care for Royce Jr. and also helped Royce Sr. with the farm chores. It was a satisfactory arrangement for all concerned.

Anthony's plan was for his family to arrive by Christmas, but shortly after Labor Day his wife wrote and told him she'd changed her mind. She was not leaving Coventry, this year or ever. The pictures he'd sent her had frightened her and the children. She had a job in an office, and she was not about to move to the depths of "Sherwood Forest."

Anthony called and wrote, but his wife was adamant. She hoped he would come home. By Thanksgiving, he decided to leave for Coventry on December 1.

Margaret helped him pack his bag. She was tempted to go with him. As much as she loved Royce, life in this strange place, surrounded by people who did not hide the fact that they considered her a "foreigner," was more than she'd bargained for. Many times it was implied that Royce should have come home and married a local girl.

On December 1, after a tearful goodbye, Margaret watched Anthony walk to the pickup that would take him to Knoxville. She dried her tears, and resolved to do what Royce's mother was always telling her: "You made your bed, now lie in it."

Shortly after one o'clock the sheriff knocked on the Lamberts' door. Margaret feared it was bad news even before she opened the door, and it was. Anthony had been killed instantly when the pickup in which he was riding collided with a dump truck near the Greyhound bus station. His body had been taken to the city morgue. The drivers of the pickup and dump truck were seriously injured, but alive.

On December 3, Anthony was buried in the community cemetery because there was no money to pay for a return to Coventry.

The cemetery was visible from the kitchen window, and at dawn the morning after Anthony's burial Margaret saw him walking out of the cemetery gate carrying his bag. Her heart almost stopped. She ran out of the kitchen, but by the time she reached the back porch he was gone.

Common sense told her she'd seen a ghost. Back home in Coventry ghosts were part of the fabric of everyday life, and she'd heard Royce's family talk about them, but this was her first such encounter in America. When the shock abated a bit, she walked to Anthony's grave. The flowers were wilted, but otherwise it was just as she'd last seen it.

Perhaps, she reasoned with herself since she felt no fear, she was probably reliving a vivid memory. It seemed normal to speak to him. "Anthony, I know you wanted to go home to Coventry. If I saw your spirit this morning, I hope you're there by now."

During the next few weeks she saw Anthony several times. As the years passed she saw him less frequently, but she and many other people saw luminous figures and lights in the cemetery. Nobody seemed overly excited about it, and said there was usually more activity after a burial.

Author's Note: I met Margaret, who told me this story, at a wedding reception in a local Methodist church. The bride had arrived in America from Russia a week before the wedding, and she spoke very limited English. Empathy for what probably lies ahead for this young woman prompted Margaret to share her story. She asked me not to use real names, because her husband's family might be hurt.

Margaret said that as tough as it was to adjust to life in Sevier County, she and Royce have shared a happy life.

They have moved away from the house beside the cemetery, so she rarely sees Anthony, but she believes he still wants to go home.

Chapter 15
Revenuer Still on the Job

Will Murphy is the son of a Northern man, Corburn Murphy, who had opened a store near the town of Gatlinburg, Tennessee, in 1939. The family lived in the back part of the store, so Will and his siblings were in the store from the time they could walk.

Along with learning his ABCs, Will Murphy learned about how moonshine whiskey was made, consumed and sold. Corburn had consignment arrangements with moonshiners to help them sell their whiskey.

Corburn would sample moonshine, but never got drunk. He quickly adopted the local practice of using it to treat himself and his family. When a Murphy was ill, a concoction of whiskey, black pepper, and honey was the favorite remedy.

Will Murphy tells many vivid stories of life in the Great Smoky Mountains before Gatlinburg became a tourist mecca, but none sends tingles up spines like his account of Rayfield Howell, the phantom revenuer. Fate led him to the time and place where Rayfield Howell would die, and he has seen his ghost many times. He's lost count of the number of other people who say they have seen him.

He appears most often at the sites of moonshine stills, and where "blind tigers" once stood. "Blind tigers" were roadhouses or bars that sold the illegal brew.

The first report Will heard about the phantom revenuer, after he had seen Howell's ghost himself, was from a moonshiner who was running a still in Jones Cove. A couple of wild hogs had been seen in the area, and when he heard a sharp rustling in the leaves he picked up his shotgun to take a look.

Wild hogs are passionate about still-slop, and can smell it for great distances. They must be kept away or they will destroy the still in trying to get at it.

The moonshiner saw no wild hogs, but he found himself looking straight into the barrel of a revenuer's shotgun. The revenuer was in the shade, but he looked odd, and said nothing. The moonshiner knew the revenuer had the drop on him, but he figured it was shoot or be shot. He stared at the revenuer, but before he could fire the revenuer simply faded away.

After hearing this report, Will suspected the moonshiner had seen the ghost of Rayfield Howell. Subsequent sightings have confirmed the ghost's identity in Will's mind. Howell was a feared and hated revenuer.

The mountain men who made whiskey considered themselves "blockade runners," and their business was to get their product to market through the United States government blockade without paying taxes on it. The terms "moonshine" and "moonshiners" were coined by the government revenue officers sent into the mountains to collect the taxes on the whiskey and destroy the moonshine operations of those who refused to pay.

Blockaders/moonshiners held the government revenue officers in great disdain, and called them "revenuers." The revenuers were paid a fixed rate for each still they cut up and the number of moonshiners arrested. The inevitable result was open, bloody and deadly warfare between the moonshiners and revenuers.

Will was about sixteen when a moonshiner asked him if he'd like to make some money helping him and his partners run a still. His father didn't object, since he had completed the highest grade offered in the only school in the area, and he had other children to help him in the store.

On the morning of his first day at the new job, Will and two men picked up sacks of sprouted corn that had been ground by a miller, and started on the trek to the still. Two hours later they arrived in a clandestine gulch, considered to be beyond the prying eyes of anyone who might inform the revenuers, as well as the eyes of the revenuers.

The gully was so choked with laurel, briers and rhododendron that it was impossible to get through the opening the moonshiners had hacked without getting jabbed. Will was over six feet, but strong and skinny. At some points he had to crawl on all fours. The still was in a small clearing with a spring that supplied the water required.

The ground corn they'd carried was dumped into boiling water to make "mash." This would take several days, so the trio headed home.

They were nearing the Murphy store at twilight when shots rang out from a house below the road. The three men jumped out of the road and dropped to the ground. The two moonshiners drew their revolvers. Will was unarmed.

Within seconds a mob of about fifteen moonshiners, some armed with rifles, had surrounded the house and were firing through the windows. Will saw two men tumble out of a side window, and so did one of the mob. He let out a yell, and the mob ran toward them like a swarm of bees.

What was happening was clear to the trio lying on their bellies. The mob had captured two revenuers, but the revenuers were armed with pistols and somehow managed to fire before the mob reached them. There was more gunfire. When it ceased, the two revenuers were prone on the ground. The mob leader ordered a couple of the moonshiners to drag the two revenuers into the nearby thicket, and told the others to go home.

Will decided on the spot that he did not want to be on either side of the moonshine war.

The next day, Will heard a moonshiner tell his father that when he and another man had gone back to dispose of the bodies, they were gone. This was the subject of conversation for several weeks. Some thought the revenuers had been eaten by wild hogs who roam the area. The biggest mystery was that nobody had seen what happened to the bodies, or was not telling.

It was over a year before the mystery was solved. The two revenuers, Rayfield Howell and Sam Black, had survived their wounds. After the mob left, they made their way to a nearby pasture and pressed two mules into service. They got to another revenuer's house before daybreak.

The revenuer and his wife treated the two men, but Sam Black died the next day. The revenuer took Rayfield Howell to a hospital in Knoxville, and he was released a few weeks later with a mended body and a bent for revenge.

During the next five years, Howell went after moonshiners with a vengeance. He found arrests bothersome, and besides he got paid the same amount for a dead moonshiner as he did for a live one he arrested. He chopped up the stills for an additional payment.

Will Murphy came to know Rayfield Howell by sight, and he secretly admired the man.

On Christmas Eve, he and his brother were squirrel hunting when they came upon a small still under a rough log shelter. No one was in sight, but being wise in mountain ways, they knew it was prudent to move along.

There was a movement in the brush, and Rayfield Howell stepped out with a shotgun pointed at them. He demanded to know if this was their still. Will and his brother proclaimed loudly and firmly that they had nothing to do with the still, and showed him the squirrels to support their alibi.

Howell had lowered the shotgun when a bullet whizzed through the air and into his heart. He died instantly. Moments later, a voice from the bank above the still suggested that the hunters get back to their squirrel hunting. They did.

The next year, Will was squirrel hunting in the same area. Howell again appeared with a shotgun pointed at him. Will knew Howell was dead, so as he felt the hair on his head stand up he calmed himself by admitting he was seeing a ghost. He called out, "Mr. Howell, I'm just a squirrel hunter. We met last year."

Rayfield Howell evaporated. Will has used this line every time he's encountered Howell's ghost, and has not felt any fear since the first encounter.

Hikers have seen the phantom revenuer walking on hiking trails with a shotgun under his arm. Few recognize him as a revenuer, since revenuers, by and large, have faded into history. Most report that they were startled, but not frightened until he vanished before their eyes.

Chapter 16
Ghost in Our Rock House

Several years ago my sister, Jane Joyner, and I inherited a river rock house in Swain County, North Carolina. This is a picture of the rear of the house.

The house had been vacant for over two years, and in June 2004 we began major renovations. We contracted with B-Dry Inc. of Knoxville, Tennessee, to waterproof the basement. A crew of three men began the work on June 28.

The B-Dry system for this house required them to jackhammer a trench into the concrete floor along three perimeter walls. They had to cut holes in the walls that divide the rooms so they could jackhammer out the concrete to construct a continuous trench to allow the water to flow out of the basement.

Jane and I were upstairs, enjoying a lull in the jackhammering, when a terrified scream came from the basement. We sprinted downstairs, fearing someone was injured.

The three-member crew was outside the entrance door to the basement. Nobody looked hurt, but one man was slumped in a lawn chair, very pale and tense. A puzzling crescendo played across the faces of his two crew mates — hints of concern, embarrassment and amusement.

We pelted them with questions, and this is what we learned:

All three members of the crew had been down on their hands and knees cutting holes in the walls with hand tools. Jim, the one slumped in the chair, was inside a closet trying to cut a hole between the closet wall and the adjoining bedroom. The closet is so narrow that it was hard to manipulate the hand tools.

Jim said he felt someone touch him on his right shoulder, and thought one of his crew mates wanted to speak with him. He was facing the wall, and his cramped position made it impossible to look around, so he stopped work and said, "Yeah?"

No answer. Thinking something might have fallen from the closet shelf, he resumed work. Within a few seconds he felt a cold, icy grip on his shoulder, and he knew instantly that it was the grip of a ghost. He'd felt it once before, back home in Kentucky.

He screamed and started scrambling out of the closet. His crew mates were there before he got out, and they helped him to his feet. Ed and Wayne, the other two crew members, said he was "deathly pale."

All three asked Jane and me if we knew we had a ghost, and we assured them that we did not know, and had never heard of a ghost in the rock house. We asked questions as tactfully as we knew how to ascertain that this was not a prank. Ed and Wayne were emphatic that it was not.

Jim, still visibly shaken, said, "You probably think I'm nuts, but you've got one now. I *will not* go back in that room to finish cutting that hole. One of these guys will have to do it."

When Jane and I were inspecting the finished work, we asked Jim if he'd been back in the room, or been bothered by the ghost. He said he had not been back in the room, but that he had felt vibes from the ghost when he helped the other guys pour concrete, around the adjoining wall. He said, "I quit while I was ahead, and left them to it."

Photograph by Juanitta Baldwin © 2004

Author's Note: This is a true account of the happening on June 28, 2004. Two of the crew members, who experienced the ghost, are pictured above, but the names in this story are not their real names. They gave me permission to make this photograph and, write this story. I had no clue it was just chapter 1. Read on!

Noises must annoy the ghost that's hanging out in the basement. This window is in the room where Jim had his encounter.

Jane and I call it the "window to nowhere" because it opens into a tunnel under the upstairs porch. The original builder dug the tunnel so he could put windows in all the rooms in the basement.

The sides of the tunnel were not reinforced, so gravity has pulled the dirt down and filled in the tunnel so it is no longer usable. The entrances were sealed, and this window was painted. When we had it pried open, hoping to find buried treasure, the only thing we found was a clear glass gallon jug, partly filled with the red clay soil.

We contracted with a carpenter to remove the "window to nowhere" and install materials to make the wall solid. He removed the window, and reported that he heard strange noises almost all the time he worked on it, and without any further explanation terminated his employment with us.

Another Visit!

On November 3, 2004, I met R.V. Lawson, a subcontractor for Home Depot, of Morristown, Tennessee, at the rock house so he could begin installing all new windows. His regular helper could not be on this job, so his wife, Mae, had come.

R.V. estimated the job would require two and a half days. Since there was no reason for me to be on the site, after showing him around we agreed he'd call me to let me know when to return to inspect the job and pay him. He called and said he'd have the job completed about noon on November 5.

After the job had been inspected — and found to be first class all the way — R.V. and Mae told us what had happened on the two evenings they had been on the job.

R.V. had worked until dusk on both days. They turned off all the lights and starting driving away. When they'd gone about 100 feet, Mae saw lights in the basement and told R.V.

He told her it must be a reflection of some type, because he'd turned off all the lights. Mae was insistent that it was not a reflection, so R.V. turned around and went back. There were lights on in the basement. He said he went into the basement, and an eerie feeling came over him, because he remembered turning off the two lights that were burning. Nothing to do but turn them off again, so he did.

The same thing happened the next evening, but R.V. said we'd just have a higher electric bill because he was not going back into that basement that night. All was tranquil next morning, but the same two lights were burning!

Author's Note: R.V. and Mae Lawson gave me permission to write their story and use their real names. The Lawsons said they told us what happened to put us on notice that there's a ghost in the rock house!

Yet Another Visit!

The names in this story are real. On January 13, 2005, we signed a contract with Charles Headrick of Sevierville, Tennessee, to complete the work in the basement. This included sealing the hole left when the "window to nowhere" had been removed.

Charles, and his crew of three, completed the work within a month. After the contract was finalized, he told me there had been a couple of unusual events I might find interesting. "Tell," was my response!

Charles said on the first day of work, two of the crew members remarked to him that they got strange feelings when they went into the room with the "window to no-where." John Kimbrough said he just felt "kind of cold and creepy." Gary Ray said the hair on the back of his neck wanted to stand up.

Charles said he and Charlie, his son, just saw a hole in the wall that needed repairing, but didn't get any vibes. They did most of the work to fill the hole where the window had been, and make it a solid part of the wall. Even after the wall was solid neither John or Gary liked to work in that room, but did as necessary.

On February 4, Charlie went outside to turn off the main water cutoff. When he started back, he saw a man with long black hair standing in the upstairs window, looking straight at him.

 He started toward the window for a closer look, hoping the man was Gary because his hair is shoulder length, but when got close to the window the man was not there.

He returned downstairs, and keeping quiet about his weird feelings, asked Charles why Gary was upstairs. Charles replied that Gary was in the room with the "win-dow to nowhere" working, and had not been upstairs.

Charlie said, "Well, there's a man up there. I saw him."

Charles said he rushed upstairs to see if anybody was there because no one should have been. He searched every room, and no one was there. He was a bit surprised that Charlie did not go upstairs with him.

He went back down and told Charlie nobody was upstairs. At this point he seemed quite shaken, and said he felt very weird while he and the man were looking at each other, and he was glad this was his last day on this job!

Author's Puzzlement: Three different crews — from different cities in Tennessee, Knoxville, Morristown, and Sevierville — working months apart — none of whom know each other — tell us we have a ghost in the rock house.

Since the basement work has been completed, we've had no more reports about ghosts.

Jane and I wonder if the tunnel under the porch had become a ghost condo, and the residents resented the renovation noises, and removal of the window to nowhere. If so, the wall is now solid, assuring them the return of peace and tranquility!

Chapter 17
Shopping for Haunts on eBay

Aficionados of eBay spread the word that "you can find *anything* on eBay."

They've about converted me, because I found you can even shop there for haunts and ghosts! Since I've never seen a ghost, I decided to try to buy one.

The haunts and ghosts I won on eBay came in tangible objects, so they were shipped to their new home in the Great Smoky Mountains via the U.S. Postal Service.

Haunted Whiskey Jug

My first haunt made "its" home in a brown and white whiskey jug, according to the seller, Carol Bax Merchant of St Peters, Missouri, who had the jug up for bids. She described it this way:

"This unusual vintage stoneware 'moonshine' whiskey jug is quite the family heirloom. My grandfather gave it to my father, and now my father has given it to me. I don't know how old it is, but my father did replace the cork a while back.

"I have never looked inside, because the cork is very tight. I have NO desire to keep this heirloom, because of the rattling noise coming from inside the jug. I know this sounds crazy, but it gives me VERY UNEASY FEELINGS/ WEIRD VIBES! It's gotta go!"

I emailed Carol and asked for more details about the jug. She wrote:

"I am a computer graphic artist, and I spend many hours in my office. When my father gave me the jug, I placed it as decoration next to a very old school desk which is about five feet from my work station.

"I've never opened it, because the cork is very tight. Well, it's not what is inside that is scary, it's what is happening to the stuff inside the whiskey jug that is weird. I sit at my computer working, and I hear something moving around, hitting the sides.

"My father never had any weird experiences with the

111

jug, but after he inherited it he kept it in a backyard shed. So I never knew this 'haunted whiskey jug' existed until my father gave it to me.

"After I started having uneasy feelings, he told me its weird history. He remembers that his father, Sam Henry Bax, always kept this jug within arm's reach.

"Sam lived in St. Elizabeth, Missouri, population 293. The CH Corner Bar was the local saloon, and Sam visited it regularly, accompanied by his best friend, the whiskey jug I have now inherited.

"One summer evening in 1966, after his visit to the bar, he decided to work on some farm equipment. He lost an arm, and from that day on had to wear an artificial arm. Sam died in 1972, and my father, James K. Bax, became the proud owner of his father's whiskey jug."

There was my chance to see if a haunt could be transported from one place to another. I was the high bidder, and in due time my haunted jug arrived.

I emailed Carol that the jug and I were getting settled in. I had placed it beneath my computer desk, anticipating sounds. None came, so after a couple of days I thought maybe some tender loving care might make it feel at home, and it would do its normal thing.

I shook the jug, and there was definitely something in it, so I took the cork out and turned it upside down. Dirt spilled all over my desk! I cleaned up the mess, put the cork back in, put it back on the floor, and gave it a mental order to stop being mute. I thought an audible order might be offensive. I went back to writing on my computer. Moments later, I heard a very loud CLINK behind me. I whirled around in my chair, but nothing was out of place. I looked everywhere, but found nothing that could have made that clinking sound. I went back to work, thinking that maybe...

Next morning, I went out the door of my office that opens to the outside, and there on the doormat was the glass cover from the light fixture — unbroken — the CLINK!

After my report to Carol, she emailed me: "Juanitta, you are so brave. The haunted whiskey jug has found a new home, and my home has found rest...no more spiritual weird experiences."

I moved the jug to the sun porch, and it just sits there sunning itself — in stony silence!

I've bid and won three more ghosts on eBay, but so far I have only the objects the sellers said they inhabited, and not one shred of abnormal activity. This has been an interesting experiment. I invested less in it than the price of a ticket to a good show.

Over a million people shopped on eBay for ghosts and haunts in 2004. I had an interesting experience with one item I did not buy.

In 2003 a "Haunted Ghost in a Painting —World War I Era" was up for auction. The seller said she'd bought it at an estate sale, and that the great-niece of the woman who had owned the painting told her it was haunted. The man in the painting was the owner's fiance'. He went off to war, and was never heard from again.

Although she'd been warned the picture was haunted, the seller said she dismissed it as a "bundle of hooey." She bought the painting and took it home. Intense calamities started happening, and she wanted to throw it in the trash, but understands that if ghosts do exist, they are probably souls in purgatory, and throwing it in the trash would trap the soul in the painting with no chance of getting into heaven, so she put it up for sale on eBay. This was such an intriguing tale that I made a token bid on the painting.

The painting sold for $316. I was delighted when the buyer wrote and asked if I'd like her to keep me updated if she had any paranormal experiences. My answer was yes! Sometime later she wrote saying it seemed she'd bought a picture but no ghost, and asked if I had any ideas on how to establish the true history of the picture.

As a lark, I decided to delve into this mystery. With a lot of research, and the help of some writers who live in the area where the painting was up for sale, I established contact with the daughter of the woman who owned the painting. These are the facts:

1. Her mother is still living, and she does not have a great-niece who attended the estate sale.

2. She identified the man in the painting with his full name, and a brief history of his life. He was not her mother's fiance'.

3. In the 40-plus years the painting had been in her mother's home, there had been no hauntings whatsoever.

4. Her conclusion was that the woman who put the picture on eBay just needed a good story in order to sell the painting, or another customer at the auction spun the haunted yarn for the sheer fun of it.

It was a fun challenge to solve this mystery. I've given up trying to buy a ghost. If you decide to shop for a ghost on eBay — or anywhere — *caveat emptor.*

Chapter 18
Bells Toll as the Blue Moon Rises

Granny women were members of almost every community in the Great Smoky Mountains at a time when the region was isolated because its roads were for horse-drawn wagons, not motor vehicles.

Most granny women were respected because they were sources of help and comfort. They delivered babies, possessed herbal knowledge and dispensed potions to the sick. Most of them were believed to have "second sight," and at Christmas or New Year they gave predictions for the coming year that were believed and heeded.

Three major economic developments brought the outside world to the dreamy blue mountains, and were the death knell for the institution of granny women.

The first development was the railroads, built to haul coal and timber. The second was the creation of Great Smoky Mountains National Park. It began in the late 1920s, and over the next fifteen years over five thousand families were forced to leave the only homes they had ever known. The third was the creation of the Tennessee Valley Authority in 1933 to bring electricity to the region.

In the fusing mix of old and new, when granny women died they were not replaced. Their descendants, now mostly the elderly, still hand down stories about them with keen enthusiasm. This is one of those stories.

In 1927, Granny Deltie Jenkins was living in the same log cabin where she'd lived for over fifty years. She had buried her husband, and two infants, under the plum tree he planted on their wedding day. Her two sons and three daughters had married and moved away. She was an energetic and determined old woman of eighty-five, who thrived on helping those who came to her for help.

Her cabin was near Mingus Mill, a few miles from Cherokee, North Carolina. Mingus Mill was built in 1887, and restored in 1937 by the National Park Service, and is open to visitors. Granny Deltie's cabin rotted down after she was forced to move to make way for the national park.

Granny Deltie's two pleasures were dipping snuff and fishing. One June morning she was fishing in Mingus Creek when Maggie Copeland, a woman known far and wide as a "bad woman," approached her. With her gift of second sight, she looked into the woman's soul and saw that she was in turmoil. Granny nodded. The woman also nodded, and sat down a few feet away.

Maggie did not speak, but kept her eyes on the creek for several minutes, then declared firmly, "I've come to beg you to tell me how to cast a spell."

Granny Deltie looked her square in the face for several seconds. "I don't do evil spells."

"I didn't say it was evil."

"You don't have to. Your countenance shows you're holding a grudge. Maggie Copeland, when I brought your fatherless boy into the world last year, you promised to do better, but you ain't. I hear tell you give him away."

"That's a lie! My boy's daddy swears he'll kill me if I ever tell it's him, and I believe him. He took my boy and give him to some rich people in Asheville. I think they paid him a lot of money. Maybe he's better off, but I grieve for him. That's why I want a spell."

"To get your boy back?" Granny asked.

"No. I want to punish his daddy. It's not right that he can pretend, making everybody think he's a man of God when I know he's one of the Devil's best men!"

Granny Deltie was surprised, and she did not like surprises. She prided herself on knowing everything about everybody in the county, and if Maggie was telling the truth, the man she'd pegged as the daddy, wasn't the father. Her second sight did not eradicate curiosity, and a strong surge of it propelled her into action.

"If you're telling the truth, God knows you got just cause for a grudge."

Tears ran down Maggie's cheeks, but she ignored them,

staring unblinkingly at Granny. "What I said is the truth. Will you help me?"

"How do you want to punish this man?"

"I want him to suffer what you think is enough punishment for what he's done. I want him to know I am causing his suffering, just like he's making me suffer."

"You say he pretends to be a man of God. Who is he?"

Maggie turned pale. "He said he'll kill me if I tell."

"I heard that," Granny snorted, "but I have to know who he is if I'm to conjure up a spell to make him suffer. You have my word that I will not tell his name to anybody, except if I cast the spell I will tell him that it is because of his dastardly deed. He will know you told me."

"Preacher Bradley Enloe."

Granny's second sight confirmed that Maggie was telling the truth.

"Tell me how it happened."

"I was walking home from school on the Spillcorn Trail. Preacher Enloe rode up behind me on his horse, and asked if I'd like to ride, since it looked like a storm was brewing. I saw he was riding bareback, so I said yes. He helped me up and we rode along for a little way, but he did not say anything. When we got to the prong in the trail that goes to our house, he took the other prong, so I said I'd best get off and walk, since he was not going by my house.

"He said that there was a hanging rock just down that prong where we could wait out the storm. It had started to rain, and there was thunder in the distance.

"By the time we got to the hanging rock, it was raining cats and dogs. He helped me down and tied the horse to a tree. Do you know where this rock is?"

"I do. You ought to know it's a praying rock. Don't you know that preachers and granny women like myself place one or more little rocks near the hanging rock to stand in for the person we are working with?"

"You know my family's not much for praying. I've seen the little rocks but didn't think much about it. Anyways, now you know where the deed was done."

Granny asked, "Were you agreeable?"

"No! I tried to get away, but he was too strong. He held me down so hard I had bruises all over me. When he let me set up, he told me he'd kill me if I ever told, and besides, he said with an evil grin, nobody would believe me. That grin told me he'd enjoy killing me, just like he'd enjoyed making me a bad woman. I lied to Mama about my bruises, and I took several whippings from Mama and Pa because I would not tell who got me in the family way."

Granny said, "Preacher Enloe put up most of the money to build that little church on yon side of Mingus Mill. Tell me about how he took the baby."

"He come by the house a week after my boy was born, and told Mama and Pa that he'd come to pray with them because he'd heard of the disgrace I'd brought on them. Pa was quick to tell him that sympathy without relief was not worth a damn. Preacher Enloe said that he agreed, and he'd

120

not come empty-handed. He pulled some pictures out of his pocket and handed them to Pa. Then he said for Pa and Mama to take a look at these fine people. They live in Asheville, and God has not seen fit to bless them with children. He said that God withholds children from people like this so they can take care of bastards brought into the world by sinners.

"Pa and Mama got the drift right off, and so did I. Lord knows I'd be lying if I said I wanted that boy, but after I held him and nursed him, I'd put that awful time under that rock out of my mind, and told my boy it was not his fault, and I loved him. I started to cry, and that made Pa mad.

"He yelled at me. Mama never defies Pa, so it was agreed that Preacher Enloe would come back for my boy in a month. He'd get bottles and clothes from the people in Asheville, and it all went off just like he'd said.

"I will never forget the day Preacher Enloe took my boy. He brought a big basket and Pa put my boy in it. As he turned to go down the steps, he asked me to help him put the basket in his wagon. I was sobbing, but nobody paid any attention. He didn't need me to help him put the basket in the wagon; he wanted a chance to threaten to kill me one more time if I told.

"I knowed he was right. Who'd believe me? I still think he got paid a lot of money, and I know in my heart he's done this before, and will do it again. Granny Deltie, tell me true, don't you think he deserves to suffer?"

"Yes, and he will suffer. It's justice."

"Tell me how to throw a spell on him."

"Child, don't be foolish. Throwing spells and curses is just part of mountain magick, and it takes years and years to know how to grab and use the words of power. I'll gather what I need, and if you swear you will take this secret to your grave, by the next blue moon you will know Preacher Enloe is suffering."

"I swear!"

The first time she saw Preacher Enloe, Granny Deltie saw that he had a black soul, and that their paths were doomed to cross. Maggie had brought doomsday to her.

She'd met Preacher Enloe on the road close to her house the previous week. She was carrying six rainbow trout she'd caught that day. He remarked on her bounty, and invited her to attend services at his new church.

"Where'd you get such a fine bell?" Granny inquired. "I can hear it from my porch."

"A blacksmith in Cherokee made it."

"You gonna use it to chase away ghosts, evil spirits, and them Nunnehi Indian fairies?"

Preacher Enloe was horrified. "Indeed not! Mingus Chapel is a Christian church. That bell will be rung to announce services, and when somebody dies we'll ring it once for every year that the departed lived."

Granny Deltie set about gathering the things she needed for the spell. Knowing he was a selfish man, he would take and touch the things she offered. In strict obedience to mountain magick, she handled them over and over to charge and enchant them.

When she was ready, she walked to Mingus Chapel just before dark on the night before the next blue moon. Preacher Enloe was sitting in an oak rocker in front of the chapel.

"Howdy, preacher."

He stood. "Howdy, Granny. First time I've seen you here. Is anything the matter?"

"No. I caught a whole passel of fish right up the creek, and thought you might like a mess."

"I would indeed. Not being married, I have to cook for myself, and I've learned to fry fish."

Granny handed him the fish and a cloth bag. "There's some hog grease and corn meal in the bag for you to fry them in, and a few dips of snuff. I notice you dip. Nothing like a dip after a good meal."

"I'm obliged to you."

"Since I know the chapel bell will toll for you during next blue moon, I thought you might as well have some pleasures."

Preacher Enloe dropped the bag as if it were a hot poker. "I've been told you're a witch! Are you trying to put a curse, or an evil spell, on me?"

Granny Deltie smiled. "I hear tell you're thirty-five years old. If you go to the praying rock on the trail near

Maggie Copeland's house, you will see a closed circle of thirty-five rocks. You know why. Now you know you will suffer to pay for your evil deed. The bell will toll for you."

The next night, as the blue moon climbed into a cloudless sky, the bell in Mingus Chapel began to toll. Neighbors rushed to the chapel to see who was ringing the bell, and to find out who had died.

Bill Walker and Floyd Phillips arrived first. They stood transfixed, trembling with fear, at the site of a ghostly witch ringing the bell. It faded away before anybody else arrived, but the new arrivals, witnessing the condition of two rugged men with a reputation for not being afraid of man or beast, believed what they were told.

Somebody regained enough wits to ask if anybody had seen Preacher Enloe, and everybody said no. A search began, and they found him dead on the creek bank.

Chapter 19
Jenkins Mill Ghost

Jenkins Mill on Highway 19, in Swain County, N.C.

During the 1930s, my great Uncle Charlie lived in the home of Sally Jenkins, and worked in the Jenkins Mill.

He and my grandmother, Mary Burchfield Stallcup, one of his younger sisters, were very close. She'd take about half a bushel of corn to the mill, along with some of his favorite foods, and they'd visit. She also took on the hopeless job of squelching rumors about Charlie and Sally.

I heard this story from my grandmother after Charlie had gone to his reward. He'd made her promise not to tell anybody while he was alive, because he didn't want people to think he, Charlie Burchfield, was crazy.

Uncle Charlie told Grandma that one hot day in July he was doing a maintenance walk on the millrace. Water entered the millrace on a heavily wooded steep mountain and continued downhill until it reached the mill. Each year the undergrowth had to be cut back on each side of the millrace, and downed limbs and other debris had to be removed from the water.

There were several mountain laurel thickets on top of the ridge behind the mill. On this day, Uncle Charlie heard unusual sounds coming from a thicket. His hearing was not as keen as it had been, so he could not tell whether the sounds were from an animal or a human.

He stepped into the edge of the thicket to hear better, and called out. There was no direct response, but the sounds continued. Knowing how dangerous it is to get entwined in a laurel thicket, often called a laurel hell, he continued on up the ridge. On his way back, he heard the sounds again, but this time he kept going.

The sun was setting, and he wanted to get back to the mill before dark. When he'd gone about fifty feet past the thicket, he saw what looked like a flash of lightning. The woods were so thick that it was impossible to see the sky, but there was no wind and no thunder.

After this flash, he heard the same sounds he'd heard coming from the thicket. He stopped, retraced a few steps and looked around as best he could in the growing twilight. He saw nothing unusual, so he walked close to the millrace for several minutes, thinking maybe an animal had gotten trapped in the water. There was no animal, but he did see something white floating in the millrace toward the mill, a few feet beyond his grasp.

He saw tiny circles of light over the millrace, but thought this was the reflection of the setting sun on the flowing water in the millrace.

Although he'd been puzzled by the unusual events, Uncle Charlie said he did not feel uneasy, and made his way back to the mill without anything else out of the ordinary.

It was dark by the time he reached the mill. He checked the doorway to see if anybody had left a turn of corn while he'd been gone. No one had, so he did not go into the mill, but went home for supper. He mentioned the unusual sounds to Sally Jenkins and her brother.

They speculated about it, and joked that it might be the ghost of old man Silas Jenkins, who'd owned the land at one time and had a reputation for issuing exit invitations to trespassers with a shotgun. After he died, a hunter swore he'd seen him, and the tale took on a life of its own.

At sunup the next morning, Uncle Charlie walked to the mill. Remembering the white object he'd seen, he checked to see if it was lodged against the sluice gate, but it was not. He opened the gate to divert the water to turn the wheel to begin another day's work. T.I. Hughes pulled up in front of the mill. Uncle Charlie walked over to the wagon and was surprised to see it was not loaded with corn.

T.I. asked Uncle Charlie if he'd heard the awful news, and he said he had not, so T.I. told him what had happened during the previous afternoon.

Douglas Messer's daughter, Sadie, had shot herself with a shotgun and died instantly. Best anybody could tell why was that the man she was expecting to marry had been killed during a robbery at the bank where he worked.

Her family said that late that afternoon she threw her wedding dress over her arm and headed for the ridge above the mill. Her mother followed, frantically calling to her to stop and talk.

Sadie did stop and sit when she reached the millrace at the top of the ridge. Her mother was out of breath, but she sat down beside Sadie and hugged her. Sadie had not spoken a word, or cried a tear, since the sheriff had told her the sad news.

After a few minutes, Sadie got up and threw her dress into the millrace, and would have climbed in if her mother had not been strong enough to restrain her. After a struggle that left both of them exhausted, they went home. Sadie went upstairs, and minutes later the family heard the shot-gun blast. She'd taken her father's shotgun from the rack over his bedroom door, walked out on the upstairs porch, and had taken her own life.

The Messers lived within sight of the mill, and Uncle Charlie knew Sadie and all the children, because on hot days they'd come and play in the mill pond when the wheel was still. Sadie had outgrown this pastime, but she was always friendly and polite when they saw each other.

Uncle Charlie said an awful feeling came over him, and he now knew that the white thing he'd seen in the millrace was Sadie's wedding dress. He felt real fear that the lights he'd seen had flashed at the moment of her death.

Uncle Charlie didn't tell T.I. about any of this. No funeral arrangements had been made, and uncle Charlie told T.I. he'd walk over to the Messer home and tell the family he'd help in any way he could. T.I. said he'd drive out and tell Sally.

As soon as T.I. drove away, Uncle Charlie rushed to the sluice to see if there was any trace of the white object he'd seen, and was now sure it was Sadie's wedding dress. It was not there.

Sadie was buried three days later. After the funeral, Mrs. Messer told Uncle Charlie that Sadie had thrown her wedding dress into the millrace and tried to climb in to drown herself. She asked him if the dress had reached the mill. Uncle Charlie told her it had not, but he'd keep a lookout for it. He did not tell her about his bizarre experiences the day Sadie died.

Weeks went by and there was no trace of the dress, or any fragments of it.

People began asking Uncle Charlie if he'd been working at night, because they'd seen lights in the mill. One man asked him if he'd had a secret encounter, because he saw dim lights and a woman standing in front of the small upstairs window.

Never having believed in ghosts put uncle Charlie between a rock and a hard place. He believed the folks telling him about the lights and the woman were not lying, but he also knew that there should have been no lights or women in the mill.

He seldom locked the mill door. This was in deference to customers who might bring corn or wheat when he was not there, and the practice was to open the door and set it inside if rain appeared likely.

Each night during the next week, he made absolutely certain that there were no lanterns burning, and locked the door. Each night during that same week, after it was dark, he walked over to the mill, and every night he heard the same sounds he'd heard on the ridge the day Sadie killed herself, and saw lights. He said his hair always stood on end, and his body was ringed with goose bumps. He felt he was not alone, but never saw anything resembling a ghost.

As time went by, the stories about Charlie being in the mill became routine. He chose to take the butt of the jokes that he was having a secret rendezvous rather than tell them he'd accepted the fact that Sadie was haunting the mill, maybe looking for her wedding dress.

In early November, Uncle Charlie was walking back from having his noon meal at home when he saw a white object lodged at the top of the wheel. He dashed up to the second floor and got the long-handled hook he used to dislodge items from the wheel.

It was Sadie's wedding dress, and much to his surprise it had only a few rips and stains. He hung the dress on a rack.

After it had dried he folded it carefully and put it in a clean meal bag and took it to Sadie's mother. She was overjoyed.

Uncle Charlie was happy that Mrs. Messer had the dress, but was thankful that from that day on, all abnormal activity at the mill ceased.

Author's Note: In deference to the family who lost their daughter, their real names are not used in this story.

Chapter 20
Specter of Nance Dude

If you are in, or close by, Bumgarner Cemetery near Whittier, North Carolina, you may see a hunched, diaphanous woman who disappears when you go toward her. Most of those who've seen her believe she is Nance Dude, a woman who murdered her three-year-old granddaughter, Roberta, in February 1913.

The horrific details of Roberta's death were recorded in the local newspapers. Two books and several plays have been written that keep this legend alive. While these writings record the basic facts accurately, the authors try to explain the desperate social and economic living conditions for Nance Dude and her family that culminated in murder.

Nance Dude went to her grave at age 104 without admitting she murdered Roberta, but her possible motive emerged during her trial for murder.

In 1913, Nance was living in dire poverty with her daughter Lizzie and Lizzie's common law husband, Will Putnam. Roberta, Lizzie's illegitimate child, was the only child in the household, but Lizzie was pregnant with Putnam's child, and she hoped to marry him. He told Lizzie that he would marry her if she got "rid" of Roberta.

Putnam and Lizzie told Nance to leave his home with Roberta, and that she could not return until she had given her away. Nance wandered around the county for three days, but could not find anyone who would take Roberta. She returned to find the door locked, and Putnam yelled that the door would stay locked until she got rid of Roberta.

Nance tried again to give the child away, but could not find anyone willing to take her. She returned home and told Lizzie and Will that she had left Roberta in the county home. This was soon discovered to be a lie, and the community became suspicious that Nance had harmed Roberta.

The story goes that many people living close to Utah Mountain heard a child crying for several days and nights. Nance refused to tell anyone, including the local sheriff, where she had left Roberta. She was arrested and put in the Haywood County Jail.

On April 8, 1913, a search party of about forty people, all furious at Nance Dude, began to search Utah Mountain and the surrounding area for Roberta.

On the tenth day of a grueling search, they found her body in a cave on Utah Mountain. The entrance had been sealed with rocks too heavy for a child to push away.

Nance Dude was transferred to the Bryson City Jail because of threats from lynch mobs that had surrounded the jail on several occasions. She was later tried there and sentenced to thirty years at hard labor in the North Carolina state prison system. She was imprisoned in Central Prison in Raleigh from 1914 until 1929, when she was paroled at the age of eighty.

On May 22, 1929, a good samaritan, Aaron Hatley, recognized Nance when she got off the train in Waynesville. He offered to drive her to the Putnam cabin. Will answered her knock, and came out on the porch, followed by Lizzie. They refused to let her in.

Hatley felt it was his Christian duty to help Nance. He arranged for her to live out her days in a dilapidated cabin on Conley's Creek. He and his wife, Lois, checked on her through the years and provided limited help. Through the years, she took in several black dogs and raised chickens. She split wood into kindling and sold it.

On September 9, 1952, Aaron and Lois Hatley found Nance dead. She was one hundred and four years old. She was buried in Bumgarner Cemetery near Whittier. Most of the literature that contains this story inaccurately states that she is buried in the Conley's Creek Cemetery.

Not long after Nance Dude was buried, reports of a stooped, diaphanous ghost at the end of the cemetery began to circulate. Her grave was marked with a plain rock. There are many graves that are marked with rocks, but many of the locals know which one marks the Nance Dude grave.

Photograph by Juanitta Baldwin © 2005

One out-of-town visitor, Viola Bumgarner, who had never heard of Nance Dude until 2002, believes she saw her ghost, and photographed it. After her experience in the cemetery, she made inquiries and learned the chilling legend of Nance Dude.

Viola Bumgarner Taylor lives near Mount Sunflower, Kansas. Her major interests, since retiring as a school teacher, are genealogy and hiking. She and her husband, Shelton, have hopes of hiking each mountain in the United States that offers a 360-degree view, and they hike many miles in cemeteries, looking for links in their family trees. The Taylors don't think of cemeteries as being at all morbid, but consider them open-air reference libraries.

Viola had established that several Bumgarners had lived in Jackson County, North Carolina, and located Bumgarner Cemetery in the community of Wilmont.

They arrived at the cemetery in late afternoon on March 20, 2002. The temperature had been in the fifties, but it was dropping as clouds moved in. There was still enough daylight to look over the terrain and check a few gravestones at the outer perimeter.

There is a road through the center of the cemetery, and it took only one glance at each side to see that many Bumgarners were buried here. They decided it would take most of the next day to do a proper search.

Viola was snapping pictures across the cemetery to get an overall landscape view when she saw a frail woman in the lens. She snapped a couple of pictures and lowered the camera from her eye. The woman, who had been in focus a moment ago, had disappeared.

Viola looked through the camera lens again at the same spot where she'd seen the woman and ascertained that what she'd seen was not a shrub or headstone. She checked the lens for smudges, and there were none.

She walked to the spot where the woman had been standing, and there was absolutely no way for the woman to have walked the distance from where she was standing to the nearest trees in the instant it took to lower the camera from her eye.

Viola looked around for an explanation. Dusk was descending upon the cemetery, the river running through the valley below, and the hills and mountains beyond. Everything was quiet and serene, but her sense of internal disquiet roared. The image she'd seen had to be either a woman or a ghost

Nothing like this had ever happened to her, and she felt the tremors of an intellectual earthquake. She recalls thinking that the woman might be one of my ancestors who's glad I came, or someone who wants me to go away.

Shelton had walked toward the opposite end of the cemetery. When they met back at the car, Viola asked him if he'd seen anyone, and he said he had not.

She told him what had happened, and his response was that perhaps this was her first encounter with a ghost. The next move was to get the pictures developed. If the woman was a ghost, she probably wouldn't be in the pictures. If she was not, that would not explain how she could disappear into thin air in a moment.

This is one of the pictures on the film Viola snapped at Bumgarner Cemetery. She believes the apparition in the picture is the ghost of Nance Dude, but knows there is no way to verify her belief.

Chapter 21
Tunnel Teleportation?

This story was sent to me, and after verifying with the writer that what she wrote actually happened to her and her husband, and that it is not fiction, I am sharing it with you. The writer says:

Ted and I vacationed in the Great Smoky Mountains from March 30 through April 5, 2003. This time we'd left the kids at home with Grandma and Grandpa, so we could relax and enjoy some grown-up entertainment.

We drove from our home in Louisville, Kentucky, to Cherokee, North Carolina, and stopped at Harrah's Casino, where we lost our fifty dollars gambling money.

The next morning we drove to Gatlinburg, Tennessee, checked into a hotel near Ripley's Aquarium shortly before lunch, then spent the afternoon in the aquarium.

That night Ted called Barney and Lisa Tebolt, a couple we'd known in high school, who live in Knoxville, and they invited us to lunch the next day at the Cracker Barrel in Pigeon Forge.

Barney told us to leave Gatlinburg on U.S. Highway 441 North, and said we'd go through a one-way tunnel before we got into Pigeon Forge. After the first stoplight we should start looking on the left for the Cracker Barrel.

Ted commented to Barney that his directions were good except that we did not go through a one-way tunnel. Ted can't resist blowing the car horn in every tunnel.

This annoys me, so we'd both remember a tunnel during the short drive from Gatlinburg to Pigeon Forge. Barney and Lisa laughed and said we had to have come through it. Ted and I were positive that we did not, but shrugged it off, thinking that perhaps it was an April Fool's joke.

On Thursday we headed out of Gatlinburg on 441 to go to Dolly Parton's Dixie Stampede in Pigeon Forge. This time, we did go through a one-way tunnel, and exited it with creepy feelings. The tunnel was not creepy, but the fact that we could not remember having gone through it on April Fool's Day boggled our minds.

We still don't have an explanation for what happened to us, but we are not alone. That evening we went on a Mystery Walk at the Old Mill in Pigeon Forge, with Judy House, a professional storyteller and folklorist. You cannot imagine our relief when Judy told stories about people who have had the same experience we had involving the one-way tunnel between Gatlinburg and Pigeon Forge, and other tunnels in the park! Judy says that she has experienced it on several occasions, and it appears that teleportation may be the explanation.

I did not use real names in this story, because my friends and family back home will either laugh or think we consumed too much "moonshine" on our vacation!

Author's Note: Teleportation is the instantaneous transport of a person or object from one place to another. Scientists are working to achieve this mode of travel by combining properties of telecommunications and transportation.

I photographed this tunnel in Great Smoky Mountains National Park on February 5, 2005, after going through it — no teleportation yet, but I keep hoping!

Chapter 22
Cherokee Legend of Tsali

In October and November the ghost of Tsali, a brave Cherokee Indian, has appeared in the mists of the valleys and on the mountaintops of the Great Smoky Mountains for over 150 years.

Tsali became a legend, because the Cherokees believe he selflessly gave his life so they could remain in their beloved homeland.

In 1836 the U.S. Government secured the Treaty of New Echote that required the citizens of the Cherokee Nation to give up their homeland and be removed west of the Mississippi River to a part of the country designated Indian Territory. Although Tsali knew about the treaty, he did not become involved in the struggle until 1838.

Tsali lived with his wife and three sons in a cabin near the Nantahala River where it flows into the Little Tennessee, near Bryson City, North Carolina. He farmed and hunted to provide for his family.

One day, soldiers came to his cabin and told him that he and his family must go to the stockade at Bushnell. There they would join other members of their tribe for a long walk to a reservation in what is now Oklahoma, a walk that would go down in infamy as the Trail of Tears.

142

Tsali offered no resistance, and he, his wife and three sons started walking to Bushnell. On the way a soldier prodded Tsali's wife with a bayonet to move faster, and this angered Tsali. Speaking in their native tongue, he told other Cherokees that when he pretended to fall they should take the soldiers' guns and run for the high mountains.

The plan was successful, but a soldier was killed during the escape. This made the U.S. Army determined to recapture them, and try them for murder. Tsali and the group hid out in a cave near Clingmans Dome for months.

General Winfield Scott sent word to Tsali by Will Thomas, a white friend of the Cherokee Nation, that if he and his group would surrender they would be tried by their own people, and those found not guilty would be allowed to remain in North Carolina.

One account is that Tsali gave himself up at the home of Abraham Wiggins, a close relative of Thomas. Shortly thereafter, he was led off by his people and shot.

Another account is that Tsali was captured and executed by Euchella and Wachacha, Oconoluftee Cherokees, near Big Bear's reserve on the Tuckaseegee.

Whatever the exact details of Tsali's execution, he became a legend and inspiration. In the hearts and minds of the Cherokee people, Tsali still lives.

Author's Note: Tsali's story is told in an outdoor drama titled "Unto These Hills," every summer in Cherokee, North Carolina. Some of the actors are Tsali's descendants.

Books by Juanitta Baldwin

Unsolved Disappearances in the Great Smoky Mountains, ISBN 1880308134, nonfiction. This book narrates three types of unsolved disappearances in the Great Smoky Mountains.

Smoky Mountain Mysteries, ISBN1880308185, This book is a collection of stories about the magnificent mountains and unique people of southern Appalachia.

Kudzu in America, ISBN 1880308193, spiral-bound, in full color. This is the only book in print for the general reading public that tells the story of how kudzu came to America, about our entangled love and hate for this alien vine, and its impact upon our economy, environment and culture, and offers solutions for the problems.

Kudzu Cuisine, ISBN 1880308231, spiral-bound in full color. This is a unique cookery, using kudzu vine in each recipe in the book. There are dozens of vivid color photographs of kudzu vine and dishes prepared with it. It is written in a conversational, easy-to-read style, with stories about kudzu entwined within the recipes for a change of reading pace.